A BEAUTIFUL NEW MOVIE BASED ON
TOMÁS RIVERA'S NOVEL OF CHICANO
FAMILY LIFE IN THE 1950'S

...and the earth did not swallow him

(...y no se lo tragó la tierra)

Written and Directed by
Severo Perez

Produced by
Paul Espinosa

Starring
Jose Alcala, Rose Portillo,
Marco Rodriguez and
Daniel Valdez

Musical Score by
Marcos Loya

An American Playhouse
Theatrical Film.
Produced by KPBS-TV
and Severo Perez Films.
Executive Producers: Lindsay Law and Paul Espinosa
Director of Photography: Virgil Harper
Production Design: Armin Ganz
Editor: Susan Heick
Costumes: Yvonne Cervantes
Casting/Associate Producer: Bob Morones
Major funding provided by National Endowment for the
Humanities, Corporation for Public Broadcasting
and American Playhouse

A KINO INTERNATIONAL RELEASE

FILMMAKER'S JOURNEY

The Wittliff Collections

Wittliff Collections Literary Series
Steven L. Davis, General Editor

FILMMAKER'S JOURNEY

SEVERO PEREZ

FOREWORD BY LUIS VALDEZ

Texas A&M University Press
College Station

(∞) This paper meets the requirements of ANSI/NISO Z39.48-1992
(Permanence of Paper).
Binding materials have been chosen for durability.

Library of Congress Cataloging-in-Publication Data

Names: Perez, Severo, author. | Valdez, Luis, writer of foreword.
Title: Filmmaker's journey / Severo Perez ; foreword by Luis Valdez.
Other titles: Wittliff Collections literary series.
Description: First edition. | College Station : Texas A&M University Press,
  [2024] | Series: Wittliff Collections literary series | Includes index.
Identifiers: LCCN 2023052498 | ISBN 9781648431791 (cloth) | ISBN
  9781648431807 (ebook)
Subjects: LCSH: Perez, Severo. | Independent filmmakers—United
  States—Biography. | Mexican Americans in motion pictures. | LCGFT:
  Autobiographies.
Classification: LCC PN1998.3.P45297 Z46 2024 | DDC
  791.4302/3092—dc23/eng/20240112
LC record available at https://lccn.loc.gov/2023052498

Unless otherwise indicated, all photographs are by the author.

Cover & interior designed by Laura Forward Long

For Rafael and Rachel, my children,
who were a big part of my journey,

And for my grandsons, Wolf, Eli, and Vidal,
whose journeys have just begun

CONTENTS

Foreword, by Luis Valdez   ix

1   Production Notes: Part One   1

2   How to Make Good Home Movies   8

3   Making It   22

4   Executive Experience   29

5   *Monitos*   37

6   . . . and the earth did not devour him   43

7   Curves in the Road   46

8   Market Day   50

9   Cul de Sac   59

10   The Folioscope   62

11   Sunset Boulevard   64

12   Soldierboy   71

13   Nothing to Lose   77

14   A Day in the Life   80

15   The Right of Way   85

16   Fork in the Road   101

17   Retracing Steps   109

18   Chickens and Roosters   115

19   Circle of Contacts   120

20   Production Notes: Part Two   125

21   The Resurrection   137

22   The Wrap and Post   142

23   When We Arrive   151

24   The Way Home   155

25   Once around the Bloc   160

26   What Goes Around   169

27   The "Victory" Lap   173

Acknowledgments   177

Index   179

A gallery of images follows page 86.

FOREWORD

I enjoyed reading Severo Perez's *Filmmaker's Journey*, the memoir of his hopes, dreams, struggles, and accomplishments as a Chicano *cineasta*. I hope the book serves new generations of young filmmakers well; it is a clear and honest narrative of what it takes to survive in the film business. It is, in fact, almost a "how-to" guidebook. The interweaving of his personal experiences and feelings for his wife Judy Schiffer and family only enhances the memoir's usefulness by providing the human context of his life. He is, of course, totally entitled to interpret his own life experiences as he will. As friends and colleagues for over four decades, Severo and I have known and worked with many of the same individuals, and while my experiences have been a bit different from his, I respect his honesty and personal feelings about them.

As the book's narrative illustrates, the creation of a feature film for an independent writer/director/producer like Severo Perez is a harrowing and daunting journey from conception to projection, sustained only by the filmmaker's dogged pursuit of his own vision. The creative courage to take on Tomas Rivera's brilliant quasi-autobiographical, poetic Chicano novel ... *and the earth did not devour him*, as the subject of a "nonlinear" film, speaks to the highest level of personal dedication. In fact, the narrative spine of the memoir is the unrelenting struggle of the filmmaker, despite setbacks, obstacles, and critical reversals over eighteen years, to see his cinematic adaptation to its ultimate triumphant creation as ... *and the earth did not swallow him.*

With respect to *Zoot Suit*, *Soldierboy*, and other incidents regarding our professional exchanges, I can only thank Severo for the positive nature of his remembrances. I enjoyed working on *Soldierboy* and still believe it would make a wonderful film. The unavoidable conundrum still facing most Chicano filmmakers, regrettably, is the persistent lack of opportunity to get their projects green-lighted, often leading to unproductive competition and enmity. I acknowledge, however, that the very intensity of the art form makes the production of any feature film a potentially life-changing experience. The ultimate prize not only flourishes as a movie on the big screen but also takes root in the very soul of the filmmaker, by all evidence as an affirmation of his innate vision as a human being. In his skill and dedication, as a family man and filmmaker, Severo Perez has lived a creative life, commendable for his self-possession and integrity. In any case, I congratulate my old friend and colleague on his International Jury Prize from the Cairo Film Festival, as Best Director, as well as all the international recognitions from the Cannes, Biarritz, Havana, Guadalajara, and Moscow festivals. May his work inspire all future American filmmakers of color to aspire to global exposure. And may you, the reader, enjoy this remarkable memoir as a testament to the fiercely struggling artist within us all.

—Luis Valdez
Creative Director, El Teatro Campesino

FILMMAKER'S JOURNEY

Making a film is a lot like a stagecoach ride in the old west.
When you start, you are hoping for a pleasant trip.
By the halfway point, you just hope to survive.
—François Truffaut,
playing the part of the director, Ferrand, in the film *Day for Night*

1

PRODUCTION NOTES
PART ONE

Wednesday, April 29, 1992, wasn't a normal day. This was the first week of production of . . . *and the earth did not swallow him*. I'd been thinking about and planning to make this film for eighteen years. In 1990, my KPBS–San Diego coproducer, Paul Espinosa, and I won a major grant from the National Endowment for the Humanities to introduce the American public to literature by adapting a book to film. Tomás Rivera's cherished book, . . . *and the earth did not devour him*, which was in wide use in classrooms from California to Florida, was my film. It had taken two years to raise the additional funds we needed, but we had finally gotten the green light. On April 29, Paul Espinosa, who lived in San Diego, wasn't in town.

That afternoon, actors clutching their résumés and headshots queued in the stairwell leading to the second-floor production office. The phones rang continuously. We were doing auditions of one-day acting parts every ten minutes. The workday was interrupted by the breaking news that the jury had acquitted the four policemen in the Rodney King trial. I was disappointed that here was another example of white cops viciously administering summary punishment, and they'd gotten away with it, again. We got back to work.

That evening, I watched live TV broadcasts of frustrated youth congregating at the intersection of Florence Avenue and Normandie Avenue in South Los Angeles. For a half hour or so, people held up makeshift signs calling for drivers to honk. I didn't see it, but something sparked a change. The protest deteriorated. Young men began setting trash cans on fire, then alarmingly throwing rocks at passing cars. The live TV helicopter coverage drew more men into the streets. As evening set in, the scene metastasized to arson, to looting. A white truck driver who had made a wrong turn was dragged from his big rig and viciously attacked with a concrete cinder block to the head. All of this was caught live, for all of LA to see, over and over.

My expectation was that the situation would be policed immediately and things would go on as before. I had a lot on my mind. Besides casting, I had crew people to interview, locations to scout, and hundreds of other details to keep track of.

Thursday morning April 30, I assumed the previous night's violence had been an aberration. My teenaged children, Rafael "Rafi" and Rachel went off to school, and my wife, Judy, went to work.

For the preproduction period, I had taken over Bob Morones's casting office in Hollywood. This would be our staging area until the beginning of principal photography. The building was a semi-moderne vestige of Hollywood's glory years. The first floor had a ninety-nine-seat theater with two rehearsal/classroom spaces; the second floor had a small reception area, a main office, and two rooms for production and accounting.

I loved this part of Hollywood. In this neighborhood a modest bungalow could be the LA production office of a major New York ad agency. Nearby were CFI Film Lab, TODD-AO Sound, Technicolor Lab, soundstages, and numerous small businesses connected with the motion picture industry. Walter Lantz Productions (Woody Woodpecker) was on the corner. Over the years I had done business with many of these services. The down side? Parking on the street was grab-as-catch-can.

I'd known Bob Morones since 1981. We met on the set of *Seguin*, the KCET, National Endowment for the Humanities (NEH), and American Playhouse production, written and directed by Jesús Treviño. We stayed in touch and worked together over the years. Bob was an ace casting director and an excellent production hand. His casting director credits included *Platoon, Salvador, Romero, El Norte*, and numerous TV series.

Between auditions, Bob turned on the television. The same video segments from the previous night were repeated over and over. We were still casting one-day parts and were surprised that as the day wore on, calls from agents and actors scheduling auditions slowed considerably.

Gisele MacKenzie, a famous actress-singer, arrived for her audition as scheduled. I recognized her as one of the stars on *Your Hit Parade*, a 1950s TV musical review of the week's popular music hits. Dressed befitting a star, Miss MacKenzie made her entrance in a cloud of perfume that overwhelmed the room. Her vita stated she sang, acted, and designed custom fragrances.

She settled elegantly into our good chair and said, "There were buildings on fire as I drove north on La Brea all the way up to Pico." What? Bob and I looked at each other.

For me, Pico Boulevard was Hollywood's southern border. Miss MacKenzie didn't appear troubled. She calmly did her audition. I thanked her for coming. I mentioned I had been a fan of *Your Hit Parade*. She nodded, and exited like a star.

Gisele MacKenzie's perfume triggered Bob's asthma. Gasping for breath, he pushed open a window. As he took deep breaths, I turned on the TV. "*Breaking news!*" Firefighters were called back from an active fire because of shots fired. Apparently, there were more fires than the fire companies could handle, and the flames were spreading toward Hollywood.

I can't remember what we said, but we canceled the rest of the day.

In a rush, I jotted "not right" next to Gisele MacKenzie's name. In truth, that was a lie. The perfume did her in, but what a pro. She had an audition and she drove through burning LA to get there. I had to respect her desire to keep her career alive.

Bob called actors, notified agents, and sent the staff home. He stayed at his office just in case an actor hadn't gotten the word.

I called Judy. She told me not to worry about her. Her office was only ten minutes from home. Our daughter Rachel, on the other hand, attended John Burroughs Middle School in the mid-Wilshire area, which was in the path of the oncoming fires. Rafi was at the Los Angeles County High School for the Arts on the campus of Cal State LA, on the east side of town.

I owned a yellow VW Rabbit diesel my kids nicknamed "Sunny Bunny." The VW and I were one. Normally, I could whip in and out of lanes. That day I couldn't. Traffic was too heavy, but moving. I sensed tension in the way other drivers glanced about nervously, or kept their eyes fixed on the road. I tuned to KFWB news radio to keep up with traffic.

I knew how to avoid clogged stretches of Santa Monica Boulevard by taking side streets. At 11:30 a.m., turning west onto Third Street, I saw several cars barreling toward me. The drivers were cutting people off and driving illegally in the oncoming lane. As they flew past, I saw they were holding brick-sized mobile phones to their ears.

Arriving at John Burroughs Middle School, I wasn't the only parent anxious to pick up their child. I found parking two long blocks away. The office staff was harried but efficient. I found Rachel with other students assembled on one of the outdoor ballfields.

In the time it took me to pick up Rachel, the traffic had become heavier. My back street routes still required me to use a very dense stretch of Santa Monica Boulvard.

Inching past Vermont Avenue, I saw the same drivers I'd seen speeding on Third Street. They stood outside a discount electronics warehouse holding those huge phones to their ears. They didn't look Latino or Black. They were burly white guys in their thirties, Eastern European, maybe. A half-dozen men and women loitered near the entrance. I finally got off Santa Monica and zigzagged my way home through back streets.

Thankfully, Judy was home. I dropped Rachel off and continued east. Judy had called Los Angeles County High School for the Arts and arranged for a pickup point for Rafi. At Cal State LA, Rafi jumped in the car. Avoiding the freeways, we did better on surface streets until we turned onto Daly Street, just past Broadway in Lincoln Heights. Traffic was backed up. I was trapped in the curb lane, with cars stopped in front, behind, and on the side. At the intersection ahead I could see cars heading toward the 5 freeway, blocking cross traffic. This was an exodus. We didn't move for three changes of the traffic light. At the supermarket across the street, cars were circling the parking lot. Men carrying cases of beer burst out of the exit.

A row of storefronts lined the sidewalk to my right. In the rearview mirror I saw a gaggle of teenaged boys, Latinos, approaching, grinning and acting a little goofy. They were about ten feet away from our car when one of them broke the plate glass window of an electronics shop.

Gunshots rang out, I grabbed Rafi, pulled him down and threw my body over his.

It wasn't a heroic act. I did it without thinking. As I straightened, Rafi looked up. "You hurt me," he said. I felt badly about that.

The gunshots emboldened the drivers. Cars began to move.

When I arrived home, I called Bob Morones, my coproducer, Paul Espinosa, and cinematographer Virgil Harper. Our production was on hold until further notice.

That afternoon and evening, we watched live TV coverage as the looting spread from South LA to downtown, to East Hollywood, to Pasadena. Big-box stores like Zody's on Sunset Boulevard, Sears on Santa Monica, 7–11s, Radio Shacks, and strip-mall retail stores were breeched and looted.

Fire companies had stood down from fighting commercial building fires for fear of gunfire. The police were nowhere. The air smelled acrid; the sky glowed orange. On television, video clips of looters streaming from Sears and Zody's were shown over and over. I recognized the electronics warehouse on Santa Monica and Vermont where the men with the huge cell phones had been standing. The front door had been torn from its hinges. People walked out casually carrying boxes of who knows what. Shopkeepers in Koreatown, armed with rifles, stood on the roofs of their shops.

A curfew was imposed and the National Guard mobilized. The response hadn't been timely enough. At home in Echo Park that night we heard gunshots and stayed in the back of our house away from the street.

The following morning, inch-sized flakes of ash covered the driveway, our cars, the street, our patio and lawn. We took a short walk to the crest of our hill overlooking the West Side of Los Angeles. More than a dozen towers of gray-black smoke rose high over the basin. Ashes continued to fall from the ocher gray sky.

We didn't leave the house for the next three days. Judy told me later she'd been terrified, though she'd never shown it. I reasoned that the looters were only after commercial stuff. The events may have begun with African American outrage, but the looting that followed was multiethnic criminal opportunism. I read later that over those three days, 3,600 fires were set, and 1,100 buildings destroyed. Sixty people died.

On Saturday morning, the National Guard was in place and the curfew was finally in effect. By Sunday morning the fury had ended. The
actor Edward James Olmos, followed by a TV news crew, swept broken
glass in front of a gutted strip mall. There were rumors Olmos might run
for mayor.

The city didn't instantly get back on its feet. Bus service and school
schedules didn't resume until the following Monday morning, May 4,
and then not everywhere.

I needed to return to work. On Monday, driving toward the production office, I saw National Guard tanks in the parking lot of Pioneer
Market at the corner of Sunset Boulevard and Echo Park Avenue. I hoped
our neighborhood had been spared, but all the strip malls showed signs
of damage. I passed the gutted shell of the electronics warehouse at Santa
Monica and Vermont. Storefronts were either boarded over or wrapped
with yellow crime tape. Idled National Guard vehicles were present at
major intersections.

In Hollywood, Bob Morones's building and the motion picture
commercial businesses were untouched. The corner mom-and-pop
stores were looted. It took until Thursday, May 7, for all talent agents
and others to return to work. This project was too important to me to
fall behind. I worked nights and weekends to catch up. The riot robbed
me of eight days of preproduction work. That was a setback. The schedule we were hoping to meet meant shooting in California in late August,
and Minnesota in early September, using the Labor Day break for rest
and travel. Shooting any later than mid-September in Minnesota could
be iffy. We were on the clock and only had so many days to prepare. How
the LA riot would affect the production, I didn't know. As I mentioned
previously, I had been waiting for this moment for eighteen years.

Here is an odd detail. The entire story I've related here was a selec-
tively suppressed memory. I hadn't forgotten about it. However, before
2017, if someone had asked me when the riots had taken place, I would
not have made the connection to the making of . . . *and the earth did not
swallow him* in 1992. In April 2017, I took a break from the project I was
working on and began making notes for an article I'd been asked to write
about the making of . . . *and the earth did not swallow him.* That month the
LA Times began a series of articles related to the twenty-fifth anniversary
of the Rodney King Riots. I was stunned. I have a vivid recollection of

those terrible days, but they'd been sealed in a mental box isolated from the days that followed.

While making the film I entered a media tunnel. I didn't read a newspaper or watch television. I learned a word from a Greek scholar friend, *cathexis*. It means being psychologically and emotionally invested in one's work, a fairly accurate descriptor for my state of mind.

Whether I made the connection to making the film or not, one image was stuck in my mind as symbolic of the tragic absurdity of the riots. It's a photograph by J. Albert Diaz that appeared in the *LA Times*. A boy, perhaps seven years old, steps through the smashed window of a Big 5 sporting goods store. In his small arms he valiantly clutches a long box labeled *Thigh Master*.

2

HOW TO MAKE GOOD
HOME MOVIES

I became a filmmaker by happenstance, honestly. I didn't go to film school. After graduating from the University of Texas at Austin in 1963, I had to do two years active duty with the US Navy. That's a story I'll get to later, but because I had a college degree and was an honorably discharged veteran, I qualified for a job at the Texas Employment Commission (TEC). It was actually a great job that came along at the right time. I liked the work. I liked the people I worked with. Yes, there were still a few racist codgers hanging on to their jobs, but they'd become irrelevant.

As an employment interviewer, I helped unemployed people find jobs and showed them how to apply for unemployment insurance. TEC actually did those things. Every day people told me their life stories, where they were born, where they lived, where they worked, and how much money they made. Did they have children? How many? Were they veterans? I met people at the beginning of their work lives and people retiring. I was also introduced to a reference book that contained every conceivable job category. There were even listings for motion picture cameraman and assistant cameraman. These jobs may not have existed in San Antonio, but somewhere there were cameramen working and applying for unemployment when they weren't.

The other great thing about the job was that at 5:00 p.m. on weekdays I left the work behind. For the first time in my life, I had a steady income. I bought a brand new automatic VW bug for $1,600. I rented a clean affordable apartment in an old Queen Anne house in San Antonio.

I looked at the supervisors and senior positions at the Texas Employment Commission, and I couldn't see a future for myself there. I saw a future for libraries where films could be screened on a television/phone. I even predicted as much a couple of years later when I spoke at Texas A&I University, but I'm getting ahead of myself. I had been exposed to foreign films and documentaries at the University of Texas. I began to formulate the idea of becoming a specialized librarian with access to films, photography, and sound recordings. I read an article about the future of libraries and "new media." If new media meant my idea of a phone/television, the article didn't say. I enrolled in night classes in library science at Our Lady of the Lake College. The year was 1966 and while "new media" was still to be defined, I was curious about what it might be.

I met a lovely young woman, Madeleine, in the library science department; we were married less than a year later. She graduated about the time I lost interest in library science. The areas that interested me were not being taught at Our Lady of the Lake College. It wasn't the school's fault. It graduated perfectly qualified librarians, but not what I had in mind. Madeleine looked for a job, while my job at TEC supported us.

Fine photography, by the likes of Man Ray, André Kertész, Manuel Álvarez Bravo, Walker Evans, and many others, was my reason for purchasing a 35 mm still camera when I was in the navy. The Argus C3 wasn't a fancy camera, but it was what I could afford on a sailor's pay. I began by taking photos of Madeleine, my parents, and favorite spots in San Antonio. My seventeen-year-old brother, Carlos Rene Perez, and I took a night course in still photography at San Antonio College. Carl Leib, the instructor, also taught at Lanier High School. He told the class, "I cannot teach you how to become an artist. That you learn somewhere else. I will teach you how to take a photograph and how to print it in a darkroom in the most efficient manner. Your photos will be properly exposed, and you will have a print that contains the proper balance of black and white." Mr. Leib's streamlined darkroom techniques became invaluable. The class shaped Rene's future, and the skill came in exceedingly handy several times in my life.

I'd wanted to be a writer since I was thirteen years old. At twenty-five I didn't feel I had a story I wanted to tell, not yet, anyway. One thing I did take away from library classes was that, yes, some people were reading, but many more Americans were not reading. Hollywood's sterile romantic fantasies were the de facto literature for the masses. *Elmer Gantry*, directed by Richard Brooks, gave me hope, as did the art house movies of the 1960s, the French and British New Wave filmmakers, and the masterpieces: Ingmar Bergman's *The Seventh Seal*; Jean Cocteau's *Orpheus*; Federico Fellini's *8½*; Luis Buñuel's *Los Olvidados*; and Michelangelo Antonioni's *Blow-Up*.

Underground filmmakers of the 1960s such as Bruce Conner and Stan Brakhage, among many others, were exploring narrative structures, making drug-assisted experiments, or fooling around with naked people. I thought I would like to try.

An artist friend, Bruce Williams, who was also a college instructor, was using a Super 8 mm movie camera at the time, making experiments with lights and shadows on nonmoving objects. He could shoot long takes comparatively inexpensively, with good quality. The alternative format, 16 mm, was expensive.

Bruce reminded me that a motion picture camera was the integration of two nineteenth-century innovations, the sewing machine and the photographic plate; and the chemistry and physics of still photography were the same as for motion picture photography, obvious information I'd known before, but had never connected. I don't know why that was such an epiphany, perhaps because I'd watched my mother at her sewing machine and was fascinated by the magical mechanical fingers that drove the needle to produce perfect stitches one at a time. Imagining a single flipbook, drawings stitched together with others flowing in motion. In that instant I understood how films were made.

Bruce was right about the price and convenience of Super 8, but I wasn't interested in showing films in my living room to friends. I went with the expensive option. I purchased a used Bell & Howell Filmo 16 mm camera for $125, found a restored school movie projector for $45, mailed off for a Craig editing system for $115, and ordered a projection screen from the Sears catalog for $15. I also acquired a classy antique wooden tripod for about $12. The tripod had never been used so far as I could tell. The Bell & Howell Filmo looked quite handsome mounted on the wooden tripod. I was starting my film journey with 1930s technology.

I learned how to make films from a book borrowed from the San Antonio Public Library, *How to Make Good Home Movies*, by KODAK.

It wasn't "how to make home movies," it was how to make "good" home movies. At 223 pages, it covered basic stuff, cameras, lenses, lighting, camera angles, depth of field, focusing, coverage, and basic editing. I read it and didn't memorize it exactly. Nevertheless, over a short period I absorbed the contents.

Since I had a steady job and the expense wasn't outrageous, my wife, Madeleine, tolerated my "hobby." Our marriage was at a crossroads. She was religiously and culturally conservative. I was an atheist. I no longer wanted to be a media librarian, I wanted to make the films that libraries shared and preserved.

My brother Rene, and two of his buddies, Richard Rodriguez and Daniel Llanes, and I got together on Saturday mornings. Since I owned the camera and had read *How to Make Good Home Movies* by KODAK, I was the default expert and director. Using the exposure and compositional basics we learned from Carl Leib, we experimented with whatever came to mind. The experimenting changed when we saw our first successful footage.

I wrote an outline for a story. We filmed in and around the city and the old Queen Anne house. The following Saturday, we passed around a joint and watched the footage from the previous week. We never smoked during the actual shooting. We had to pay attention.

I loved these guys. Rene took charge of the camera. From the start he was in command of focus, exposure, and composition. More than that, he was my creative partner on all those early films. Richard had a wonderfully eccentric sense of humor. Daniel took light readings with my Weston Light Meter. He had a nearly telepathic capacity to communicate with us all. We clicked as a crew. The camera followed a man (played by me) as he goes out for an afternoon walk. He gets high, watches people, and goes home. That was about it. The finished film, *Mozo: An Introduction into the Duality of Orbital Indecision*, ran twelve minutes.

I screened the film anywhere anyone would let me and made notes about at what point people laughed or fidgeted. I learned that to sustain the moment, the editing had to be invisible, the cinematography informative but unobtrusive, and the sound needed to complement the kinetic flow. I had managed to accomplish none of those objectives. In the beginning I worried someone in the audience might question why I placed the camera where I did. No one has ever asked that question.

I submitted *Mozo: An Introduction* to the New York Filmmakers Cooperative, and it was accepted. Being listed in the cooperative's catalog was similar to being listed in *Marquis Who's Who*. Nobody really knows or cares you're listed, except for a tiny few who believe it's important.

The film toured with the underground movie circuit called the *Texas Underground* that showed a selection of films. The local theater that screened the underground movies on Saturdays at midnight was a porno theater during the day. During the screening of my film, a drunk in the audience, expecting to see naked women, wondered out loud, "What is this shit?" Several of the films in the package were cleverly entertaining. The filmmakers were mostly college art instructors and artists. My film was so-so by comparison, but it was better than some. The screening made me a minor celebrity locally. More people heard about my film than saw it, which was probably for the best.

Did I make mistakes? Murphy's Law (If anything can go wrong, it will go wrong) must have had filmmaking in mind. Fortunately, I never had a production setback from which I could not recover. I embraced mistakes, agonized over and memorialized them, and swore never to repeat them. If anything, I became overly cautious creatively.

I was offered a job with a small motion picture production company, and I immediately quit the security of the Texas Employment Commission. I was going to become a filmmaker and, hopefully, get paid for it. After I landed my first commercial, there was no looking back.

I read André Bazin's *What Is Cinema, Volume I*, but never got around to *Volume II*. I accumulated a significant library of director biographies, technical filmmaking books, and I subscribed to *American Cinematographer*.

For a year work went fairly well. The *San Antonio Light* ran an article about young filmmakers hoping to make it, with a photo of Rene, Richard Rodriguez, and me standing behind my (used, but new to me) 16 mm Bolex camera. I produced and shot a commercial for Whataburger, a regional fast food chain. With a nod to *Monty Python* (the British TV series) and the Beatles (*Yellow Submarine*), the design by artist Frank Hein won a local ad agency award. I wrote and produced several other commercials, and I was cameraman on a Sierra Club documentary opposing the construction of a freeway that would obliterate a treasured park with oak trees and a spring-fed stream.

The experience taught me a critical lesson. The big players in Texas do whatever the hell they want, and their minions make certain their bosses get their way. The film screened on the local ABC affiliate during prime time, followed by a rebuttal by the powerful mayor. Inevitably, the park was demolished, the freeway built, but at that moment, I couldn't find work as a cameraman anywhere.

My wife, Madeleine, took a job at the conservative Daughters of the Republic of Texas library located at the site of "Texas liberty," the Alamo. Madeleine became increasingly disillusioned with me. I had quit my job for the unreasonable fantasy of becoming a filmmaker and was now unemployed. I wasn't going back to work with the Texas Employment Commission, either. Madeleine's library coworkers were women preoccupied with propriety and appearances, something I was surely lacking. Since leaving the Texas Employment Commission, I had let my hair grow into a modest afro. She was warned that she would end up supporting me. She had a steady job and could easily support herself. We were still young enough that our entire lives weren't wrecked. When she told me she was moving out, I made no effort to stop her. I even rented a U-Haul and moved her things. The divorce was amicable. She later earned a master's degree, took a job with a university in Boston, and remarried.

Madeleine wasn't the only person concerned about my future. Mom sent my father to have a serious talk with me. Dad didn't try to dissuade me. In fact, he told me he admired people who took risks, but I should get a haircut.

Mom wasn't opposed to my becoming a filmmaker. She was a professional seamstress; she designed and made the cool bush jacket I wore while shooting commercials. I looked the part, and appearances were important, but I'd given her plenty of reasons to be concerned. I'd divorced a nice young woman. I'd quit a good job, was currently unemployed and I looked, well, like a drab hippy. She made me a striking dashiki cut from an African fabric.

Being listed in the New York Filmmakers Cooperative catalog was what got me invited to Texas A&I to show my film. That's where I made the pronouncements that there would be hologram movies in the future, and that the telephone and television would merge to create a new paradigm. I was steeped in Marshall McLuhan's books at the time. I didn't foresee computers or the internet.

As I mentioned, the New York Filmmakers Cooperative catalog didn't give me any credibility, but it was important to someone who mentioned me to Tony Calderon, a local aspiring civil rights champion and television producer. He was putting together a deal for a TV special sponsored by Lone Star brewery. It would feature famous Latino performers, including Trini Lopez, the Lennon Sisters, Tierra (the band), Anthony Quinn, pretty girls in bathing suits, and Joe Kapp, a football player. Tony was for real. He would go on to produce *The Deadly Tower* (1975) and *Three Hundred Miles for Stephanie* (1981).

Tony's variety TV special was a gig for me, at a time when I really needed it. I was hired to fly to California and put together a crew. Grey Advertising, the brewery's ad agency, had me contact Ken Clark, a TV commercial director. He introduced me to John Morrill, the lead cameraman. The crew consisted of John, a second cameraman, an assistant cameraman, a sound mixer, and Ken Clark. My brother Rene and Daniel Llanes were hired as assistants. What surprised me was the number of equipment cases they brought. I rented a large van to haul their gear.

This was my first time working with real pros. Ken and the crew watched the rehearsal at San Antonio's Arneson River Theater with Trini Lopez, a comedian, and local musicians. Ken and the crew met to discuss how each camera would cover the acts. Depending on how Ken Clark directed them, one camera was medium close-up, the other medium wide. The extra cases held additional film magazines. The assistant cameraman could switch out Éclair NPR film magazines in less than five seconds. If one camera stopped to change magazines, the other camera kept rolling. Both cameras were linked to the sound mixer. During the filming, Ken set the mood for the audience by laughing and applauding the hosts and the performers.

For other locations John and Ken were a little wary of going out into the barrio to shoot. I don't know what they expected. Rene and I introduced them to tacos and barbecue. The San Antonio part of the filming finished successfully. John Morrill was so impressed with Rene's photography he purchased his striking black-and-white photo of a nude couple.

Tony Calderon needed me to do the legwork for the LA portion of the shoot. I traveled to LA with the director. Ken Clark told me his folks were circus people and considered noncircus people as civilians. I think he saw me as a civilian who wanted to run away with the circus. Ken had ambitions of directing a feature film, but as a commercial director he felt pigeonholed. Naturally, we talked about movies.

Ken dropped me off at the Hyatt Hotel on Sunset Boulevard. Tony Calderon was staying there, as well. We never hung out. I don't know what Tony did or how he did it, but he had to have real connections. His entourage included Sonny Fox, a TV producer and game show host, an attorney who supplied women escorts, and a shady character I suspected would do anything for Tony. Did that mean Tony was "connected?" I have no idea. Somebody with money and clout got Trini Lopez, José Feliciano, the Lennon Sisters, and Anthony Quinn to commit. The bookings were likely arranged by the ad agency. My job was to phone the agents and give them the call times.

I had a feeling my future was going to be in Los Angeles. I could be a part-time filmmaker in San Antonio, or a full-time filmmaker in LA. I had been given a glimpse of a world where everything cinema existed every day of the year. Hollywood was like a year-round Christmas store. Working with John Morrill gave me an introduction to professional cinematography at a very high level. I realized I could never be a cameraman of his caliber, and I really didn't want to be. How good was John? He retired as the cinematography instructor at the USC film school twenty years later.

We wrapped early on a Thursday. Friday would be our last day of filming. The crew and talent were notified. The location was set, equipment ordered. I had a free evening.

I was in Los Angeles for another five days. The hotel was paid through Saturday. The cameraman, John Morrill, extended an invitation to stay at his place until I returned to San Antonio. I planned to accept.

Unless you like to party and spend lots of money in bars, there wasn't much to do on the Sunset Strip. I considered driving into Hollywood and watching a movie at Grauman's Chinese Theatre. I had time on my hands, and I had one curiosity that had nagged me for years, and because I was in Los Angeles, there was a possibility I might resolve it. I had a girlfriend in college at the University of Texas: a pleasure to talk to, politically progressive, a gifted student, played Bach and Vivaldi on her rosewood recorder, and loved to sing duets in harmony. I thought Judy Schiffer was the most beautiful woman ever. After an exhilarating, amorous summer in 1963, I finished my degree requirements in August and was promptly ordered to start my active duty service with the US Naval Reserve.

Judy and I continued a passionate letter exchange. I went home for the holidays and we rekindled the ardor. In May 1964, nineteen-year-old Judy volunteered to be trained and take part in voter registration efforts during Mississippi Freedom Summer. Her last letter came from a church address in Biloxi, Mississippi.

By June, my ship was in dry dock in Charleston, South Carolina, preparing for a special mission. The officers and crew were separated and quartered in different parts of the naval base. The Southern newspapers ran daily headlines decrying Civil Rights Violence, though in reality it wasn't the peaceful protestors who were creating the violence. Police sided with the segregationists.

That month three civil rights workers, James Chaney, Andrew Goodman, and Michael Schwerner went missing in Mississippi. I felt it urgent to do something. I should have asked for leave, and I would have likely received it, but there was no quick or easy way to contact the executive officer. My work assignment was operating a tray washing machine in the base mess hall. It wasn't like I was deserting under fire. I took it on myself to go AWOL and hitchhiked to Mississippi to convince Judy to return to Texas. When I arrived, she didn't want to be rescued, and by the way, she had a new boyfriend.

Crushed, I returned to my ship to face the music. But not right away, I took a side trip to see America. That's a story for another day. Back on the ship, I told the executive officer exactly what I had done, and why. I was given a week of "Corrective Custody" in the brig, confined to the ship for three months, and busted to seaman apprentice. I had been AWOL just short of thirty days so I wasn't charged with desertion, a felony. My punishment was stern but was recorded as a minor offense that didn't go on my record.

Before I went AWOL the executive officer had freed me from lowly seaman duties because I was good at and actually enjoyed updating the ship's charts (maps). The task entailed searching *Notice to Mariners* for details about changes to ships' channels, the location of buoys, even the lights on tall buildings. When the USS *John R. Perry* DE 1034 entered any port, the charts were up-to-date. The Exec had encouraged me to apply for Officer Candidate School. However, after my escapade, maybe because I knew the charts, he allowed me back on the bridge.

It had never been my intention to miss the ship's movement. I was back in time for the special mission. What was the mission? The *John R. Perry* DE 1034 became a spy ship. An additional exterior compartment had been built on the ship's deck while in dry dock. An array of antennas bristled on the roof, and a crew of tight-lipped guys bunked with us. For over a week, late at night, the ship would turn off its engines and lights and drift as close as a quarter mile off Havana Harbor. That was the reason for the updated chart of Havana Harbor. With the radar turned off, the captain relied on the quartermaster crew to determine the ship's position. We triangulated compass readings of a lighthouse and the beacons on tall buildings, then intersected the coordinates on the chart to see which way the ship drifted.

We were told the ship's mission was to listen and record all frequencies broadcast from Havana. I wondered if the United States was trying to provoke an incident. The Cubans surely knew we were there. Without power the *John R. Perry* was vulnerable and was well inside Cuba's territorial waters.

Judy's rejection sunk me for a bit. I understood the world was changing and she wanted to be part of the change. When we last spoke in Mississippi, she mentioned that her father had been hired by an engineering firm in Los Angeles. That had been seven years ago. There were over 2,800,000 people in LA, and another several million in the surrounding cities. What the hell. I opened the huge Los Angeles phone book and searched the white pages for my ex-girlfriend's father. There was one listing for a Sam Schiffer.

I closed the phone book and took the elevator to the Hyatt lobby. The bar was uninviting. I stepped out onto the Sunset Strip. It was about 4:00 p.m. Across the street were two twenty-four-hour strip joints, advertising "LIVE NUDE GIRLS." I wasn't really interested. I had plenty of intimacy in my life. I went back to the room and looked up Sam Schiffer's number again. I didn't get my expectations up. It could be someone else named Sam Schiffer.

I dialed. After two rings I heard, "Sam Schiffer, here."

"Mr. Schiffer, did you work for Gulf Oil in Port Arthur, Texas?"

"Yes," he replied cautiously.

"I don't know if you remember me. I dated your daughter and visited you in Port Arthur before I went into the navy."

"Severo! Of course, I remember you. How are you?"

"I'm quite well, I was thinking, perhaps you might have a minute and tell me how are things with you, Goldye, Josh, Mimi and . . . Judy?"

"Are you in town? Are you available tonight? You must come and see us. I'll tell Goldye."

"I was . . ."

"Come on by, I'd like to see you. We'll have dinner. I hope the navy thing was all cleared up? Did you get my letter?"

"Yes sir, I did. Thank you. I received an honorable discharge."

"Come on by. I'll fill you in on everyone."

Sam gave me his address. Suddenly, I didn't know if I wanted to hear what happened to Judy. When someone tells you it's over, it's over. What was I doing? I looked out the Hyatt windows at the girly bars below and decided a home-cooked meal and a conversation with a man who enjoyed talking was preferable.

Sam and Goldye lived in a modern frame house perched on a hillside in LA's pleasant Highland Park neighborhood. I knocked on the door, and the instant I stepped in I saw HER sitting on the living room couch. I didn't know how to react. I never imagined how in any possible scenario I was ever going to see her again. She didn't stand or reach out her hand. I didn't extend my hand, either. At that moment, I wanted her to be dowdy with six kids. She wasn't. She looked as stunned as I must have looked.

Why was she there? There was a simple explanation. Thursday was Sam and Judy's evening to hike with the Sierra Club in Griffith Park. Sam had neglected to tell Judy I was coming because she had arrived less than a minute before I knocked on the door.

We ended up talking, and Sam and Judy didn't hike that evening. She was married, no children, and was a schoolteacher. I enjoyed chatting with Sam and Goldye. I told them about meeting Trini Lopez and Anthony Quinn. Sam wanted to know where I was staying and offered to put me up. I told them I was at the Hyatt on Sunset.

We parted. As I drove back to the hotel, I was neither melancholy nor disappointed. I had the answer to what happened to Judy. I never expected to see her again, and frankly, I was okay with it.

I worked Friday. Before we wrapped, Ken Clark gave me a book, *Low Budget Features*, written by William O. Brown. He inscribed it: "When you're ready to make a feature, here's how you do it. Good luck!" That was very kind of him. He told me, "If you are as circumspect with others as you have been with me, you can make it." I didn't know what that meant exactly, but I took it as a compliment.

I didn't have any plans for Saturday other than checking out of the Hyatt and moving to John Morrill's place in El Segundo. The phone rang. The voice on the other side tentatively asked, "Severo?"

It was her. Now what?

"I'm glad you contacted my father," she said. "Would you like to meet me at Griffith Park by the carousel and take a hike?"

Why not, I thought. The call was an unexpected turn. I checked out of the hotel and headed to Griffith Park. We met by the brightly painted carousel and hiked to Dante's Peak, a spot on a hill with a view of the vast Los Angeles basin with downtown LA in the distance. We caught up with our lives in the seven years since Mississippi.

Judy said she continued with her political activities, working with groups opposed to the war in Vietnam, and was active in the teachers' union. She was separating from her husband.

She mostly wanted to know what I was doing. I talked about my ambitions and admitted I was divorced, had relationships, nothing serious. Eventually, I hoped to relocate to either New York or Los Angeles.

I didn't make a pass. I didn't even try to hold her hand. Back at the carousel parking lot, we sat in my VW rental.

"Real lucky I made that call," I said. "It was nice catching up. You look great." She did look great.

"What if I never see you again?" She said, her eyes tearing.

What was I going to say? I'd carried a torch for seven years, enough that I called a strange phone number on the slim chance it might be her father. I had long ago accepted that she was out of my life. I couldn't be the only person who was curious about the one that got away.

"We can stay in touch," I said. "I'm still here for a few days." I gave her the phone number at John Morrill's place and my address and phone in Texas.

Driving out to El Segundo, I didn't expect anything more. I could have kissed her, but I didn't. I didn't want to start anything or interfere in her life. She lived in California; I lived in Texas. She was separating from her husband, and those things either work themselves out, or they don't. I didn't want any part of that relationship cypher.

John Morrill allowed crew people to crash at his place. Ken Clark called it the "dormitory." John's home was a high-ceilinged one-story storefront in El Segundo, California. The street side of the building was no different from other shops in the industrial neighborhood near the Los Angeles Airport (LAX). The display windows had been bricked over, and what had been the front room where customers were greeted was now a fully equipped editing room with an upright Moviola that John invited me to use. The editing room door opened to a hallway and a space with ceilings high enough for a loft John used as his bedroom. One side of the hallway had three doors to small rooms with beds. The other side of the hallway was one large room, a machine shop with a lathe and other tools. The end of the hallway opened to an expansive dining/living room area with a fireplace. All traffic into John's place passed through the rear entrance.

The dining/living room served as a clubhouse. Filmmakers dropped by, hung out for a bit, and moved on. Besides me, there were two other guys staying there. Both were writers with ambitions. One of the guys, Paul Deason, was from Dallas and had graduated from Trinity University in San Antonio. Paul and I hit it off. John introduced me as associate producer on the Lone Star Beer variety special, which gave me a bit of status because it meant I had a job. It didn't hurt that John professionally matted and framed my brother Rene's photo of the nude couple and hung it on a prominent wall in the clubhouse.

John's business partner was Erik Daarstad, a well-known documentary cinematographer. Together they owned several Éclair NPR cameras, lenses, and tons of gear. The machine shop was where they made special rigs for their cameras. John had a couple of unusual hobbies. He collected and restored Aladdin kerosene lamps and used his lathe and machining tools to make tiny gasoline motors for model airplanes.

Judy called on Sunday morning and said it was urgent we speak. She dropped by John's place about two that afternoon. We hung out in the editing room where I was working on a film using equipment I had only seen in ads. Paul Deason and the other guy staying in John's dormitory dropped by to check Judy out. When we were finally alone, she told me she had officially ended it with her husband. At that very moment, he was at their apartment clearing out his things.

For the next three evenings, Judy made the twenty-mile drive from Echo Park to John Morrill's place in El Segundo, on surface streets because she'd never driven on a freeway.

I was honest about my prospects. I told her I was blackballed by the commercial community in San Antonio. I had no money, other than what I had earned working for Tony Calderon. Relocating anywhere was not something in my foreseeable future.

My job on the Lone Star Beer special was over. I delivered John's check for the work he'd done, which made me very popular. I said good-bye to John and the guys, moved out of the dorm and checked into a motel. Judy and I were ready for time alone.

We kept in touch. Judy wanted to fly to San Antonio over the Christmas school break. I was open to it. She came and met my dog and two cats. At some point, Judy proposed that if I was seriously consider-ing moving to LA, perhaps I should pack up all my belongings straight-away, rent a truck, move to Los Angeles, and live with her.

If Judy hadn't made the proposal, I don't know if I would have pur-sued her. Once burned, and all that. Of course, I still loved her. The offer felt right. I was ready to leave San Antonio. In three days, we packed up all my belongings, rented a truck, said goodbye to friends, and stopped by my parents' house.

Mom was terrified for me. I know that she visualized me careening down Interstate 10 in a U-Haul truck with my VW Bug dangling in tow, dangers at every turn. Dad wished me luck.

On January 2, 1972, Judy and I, Omar, my dog, and Sam and Huey, my cats, arrived in Los Angeles.

3

MAKING IT

What I learned from my first shoot in Los Angeles was that while I had basic skills as writer, director, still photographer, cameraman, and editor, none were marketable in LA, not yet. There were people in Hollywood who'd been nominated for Oscars in those crafts, and they were looking for work just like me. However, what I did know about the different stages of production put me ahead of much of my competition. What I could do that most of my competition couldn't, or didn't want to do, was budget.

Budgeting required that you know all the steps of a production. After that, the process was fairly simple, but tedious. Every scene in a script had to be broken down into its logistical elements. There was a price tag on everything, from the cost of the actors, the rates for the crew, and the price for copies and paper clips. It helped that printed budgeting forms were available at Enterprise Stationers with every conceivable budget item. Equipment rental houses such as F&B Ceco and Allen Gordon Enterprises provided catalogs with prices for 16 mm and 35 mm cameras, lenses, lighting, and grip equipment.

Dan Bessie was the first producer to give me a chance. Fifty years later, we are still friends and collaborators. Dan was an acquaintance of Judy Schiffer, the old flame soon to be my wife. He allowed me to use a desk in his office to make calls and try to land work.

I wasn't without a résumé. My demo reel had the film I shot for the Sierra Club, the Whataburger commercial, and a three-minute experimental film. Dan Bessie called them "crap," but the reel showed that I could put together a project from start to finish, just not by the professional standards in Los Angeles. The Whataburger commercial did show promise.

Dan had a long career in the animation industry doing Saturday morning cartoons and TV commercials. He started his own production company, the Learning Garden, to give himself the independence he craved. He produced educational films, including the tender award-winner, *Meet Lisa*, about his daughter with a degenerative brain disorder. Dan's TV commercial for a company that sold soft water systems annoyed viewers for years. A woman with a distinct Bronx accent yelled, "Hey, Culligan Man!"

The first job I landed was not for Learning Garden. I was hired by the Santa Ana School District TV station to write a script about one of the district's programs. I was given the particulars that needed to be addressed and I wrote a script. I thought I could pull the writing job off because my new partner, Judy, had a master's degree in elementary education and as a teacher herself was familiar with the educational programs and subject matter. However, the script I wrote wasn't the issue. I met a heavy racist vibe from the TV station's cameraman. Everything I did was under critical scrutiny. I brushed him off. He wasn't a threat and wasn't that good a cameraman, either. However, his reaction to me was a warning sign of something deeper. The Latino population in Santa Ana, California, had grown, and demands for accommodations such as bilingual education had been met with hard resistance by a faction of white administrators. I had been brought in from the outside and dropped between two warring parties. I did the best I could and was glad when the job was done. Unfortunately, the experience foreshadowed things to come.

I was fortunate to be at the right place at the right time. In the summer of 1972, Dan Bessie landed a contract to produce four educational films and needed help with budget and breakdowns for the live action sections. I made a sincere effort to help. I did a schedule breakdown for Dan and recommended for crew John Morrill, cinematographer, and Paul Deason, sound mixer, the Texas guy who bunked at John's dormitory. The combination turned out to be a good fit for everyone. Since I had already put together Dan's schedule and budget, I landed my first gig as a production manager. It was a big challenge, four 12-minute educational films with actors and animation. I was in over my head.

To the rescue came Ken Clark's gift, the book *Low Budget Features.* The same filmmaking rules apply whether making a nonunion educational film or a union feature film. The author recommended knowing the union contracts. I read the Screen Actors Guild (SAG) contract cover to cover and enough of the IATSE (International Alliance of Theatrical Stage Employees) contract to understand what to expect from cast and crew regarding hours, meal breaks, overtime, and penalties.

It's odd how the world goes round. The director of the four films was Buck Pennington, a successful TV commercial director. Buck was trying to break into longer-form TV, and these four short films had actors in scripted sequences.

When working on a set with talent that he only saw for a few moments, Buck would make up a name for them. A man wearing a red bandana became "Cowboy." Unfortunately, he called a Black actress "Geraldine." Geraldine was a female character created by the popular male Black comedian, Flip Wilson. The actress walked off the set. She closed her eyes, took several deep breaths, then came back and did her scene. Buck never understood what he had done wrong.

When Buck directed, his precise hand gestures reminded me of a dancer's. He was capable of getting uncanny performances from nonactors. Every sequence ended with a signature "button," as he called it. No one just walked down the street. There had to be a reason for the walk, and there needed to one last bit of "business," the "button," that ended the sequence.

Buck barely tolerated me. He saw me as a pain-in-the-ass newbie who brought bad news from the producer, Dan Bessie: "We (meaning you, Buck) need to speed it up," or "The crew is going into meal-penalty." His icy stares could sting.

The job was actually going well. The dailies were looking great, and we were on schedule and under budget. We had one small disaster: the assistant cameraman accidently fogged a roll of film. I didn't have to do anything. John Morrill fired him and there was a new assistant in the morning. Did I encounter racial pushback from the crew? The key grip, a good-ole boy, kept calling me "Hey, Pancho," and I was to respond, "Hey Cisco," like the 1950s Duncan Reynaldo and Leo Carrillo TV series. He was trying to get my goat and I wouldn't let him. I could have made it

about me, but he was important to the crew, hardworking and compe-
tent. The work was getting done.

One day during lunch break, Buck and John Morrill were talking
about how they got into the business. Their mutual friend, Ken Clark,
used his show biz circus heritage in directing commercials. Buck mentioned he was show biz, too. He had been a featured skater with the *Ice
Capades*. As the lead male skater, he needed an exciting stunt for his act.
He perfected a forward flip in motion and had the scars on top of his
head to prove it.

"Buck," I interrupted his story. He gave me that cold stare. "When I
was sixteen, I worked as an usher at the *Ice Capades* at the Joe Freeman
Coliseum in San Antonio, Texas. I saw seven performances of a sen-
sual duet to the throbbing rhythms of Ravel's *Bolero*." I looked at John
Morrill. "That was you, wasn't it?"

Buck grinned and almost in tears took my hand. It had been lifetime
ago. After that, Buck became tolerant of a first-time production manager.
I had been an usher at one of his starring performances. That was almost
like show business. He was responsible for getting me hired on other
nonunion shows where he was directing. As for the "Hey Pancho" key
grip, when I hired him to work on my next job, and he realized I was writing the checks, he started calling me Mr. Perez. I told him to call me by
my first name. We reverted to military style and used last names only. He
approached me once to say he hoped his grandson could see some of the
films we worked on.

If you earn respect from the crew, meaning working them decent
hours, having meals and breaks on time, doing interesting work, and
writing checks that clear the bank, the best crew folks will be available
when you need them.

One final thing about Buck Pennington, when we worked together
again, a competing producer had humiliated him with a malicious practical joke. Buck was furious and wanted revenge. Our boss, a shrewd experienced producer, warned, "I know this guy. He's spiteful. If you try to
get even, he'll only come back at you even meaner. You can't make him
go away, so you have to learn how to go around him." That was a bit of
advice I learned to apply to certain individuals I would encounter in the
business.

Those early years weren't always smooth-going, and most often it had nothing to do with race. I encountered plenty of professional enmity. As I was inventing my way through Hollywood, I met desperate souls. For them a gig meant the difference between making the rent, child support, alimony, or eviction. Cocaine was popular. Two men I met along the way ended up suicides because of pressures related to their addictions.

Every year, a new crop of piranhas (film school graduates) was released into the Hollywood pond, all of them ready to make the next *Citizen Kane*, but few with the skills of an assistant editor.

The Los Angeles Chicano filmmakers didn't welcome me like a compadre. Coming from Texas made me a foreigner and unwanted competition. Access to the few jobs available for Latino producers was jealously guarded. It turned out the local guys didn't care for each other, either. One fellow took an immediate dislike to me. Over the years he never changed. The guy had directed a documentary that was broadcast on the local PBS station, KCET.

I am proud of my birthright. I'm a Mexican American from San Antonio with deep familial Texas roots on my father's side and refugees fleeing the Mexican Revolution (1910–21) on my mother's side. I also consider myself a product of American culture: its educational system, literature, movies, radio, and television. I wasn't interested in being the "minority" hire, though I would have taken anything at that point. I came to Hollywood to make films and that's what I aimed to do. I have never denied my Mexican heritage. I knew my name could be a professional liability, but I wasn't going to change it.

The reality was that on any day on a Hollywood film set, the crew would have talented people from all over the world, including Mexican American cameramen, grips, gaffers, makeup artists, property masters. On the set, Mexican American professionals were indistinguishable from the other crew people.

In the animation industry my last name, Perez, wasn't a liability. Mexican Americans in the business included top professionals. Manuel "Manny" Perez (no relation) worked on *Bugs Bunny* and *Road Runner* cartoons and hundreds of others. Bill Melendez's company produced the Charlie Brown *Peanut* specials. Recently, Phil Roman's shop produced *The Simpsons*.

The problem was in how Mexican Americans were represented in *front* of the camera. American writers and producers were crafting familiar cop shows and sitcoms. Even the best and most progressive of producers weren't writing Mexican American characters as regulars. If a writer did write a part for a Mexican, it would often be a victim or a villain stereotype. When producers couldn't find a suitable Latino to fulfill their Latino role, they would cast a non-Latino. White actors' résumés would often list under the special skills section, "Can play Mexicans, Arabs, and ethnic types."

In the film *Battleground* (1949), Mexican-born Ricardo Montalbán played a soldier from East Los Angeles. The portrayal was positive, but the character died. I wanted to tell stories that reflected a world where men came home from war, where conflicts might be specific, but their importance universal. In 1973, as I started my second year in Los Angeles, I had no illusions about my capabilities. It was still important for me to land work on a film set and gain real practical experience.

An Armenian assistant cameraman I worked with was
reputed to have worked on Fellini's *Satyricon*.
"If you worked with Fellini, why are you here?" I asked.
"I thought I could do better," he replied.

4

EXECUTIVE EXPERIENCE

In 1973, Dan Bessie and Gary Horowitz, the CEO of Wakeford/Orloff, a production company specializing in TV commercials, secured rights to a Dalton Trumbo script, *Executive Action*, about the conspiracy to assassinate President John F. Kennedy. Burt Lancaster was to star. The hands-on executive producer was Edward Lewis. When I write "the producers" in the narrative that follows, it means Ed Lewis was speaking from on high.

I was lucky to be at the right place at the right time, again. Early in preproduction, I saw the actor who was to play Lee Harvey Oswald in costume with his props walking around the hallways at Wakeford/Orloff. I asked him if I could take his picture. Naturally, he agreed. I grabbed my camera and drove him several blocks away to a locale that somewhat matched the famous photo of Oswald holding a rifle and a newspaper. I folded a newspaper in the actor's hand and had him hold the rifle like in the photo. The next morning before the producers could hire a photographer, I had an 8 × 10 print on their desk.[1] The producer approved the work and I was hired — just not as a photographer. That was a union position.

I was offered $150 a week and gas. The photo I took of the Oswald actor became a prop in the film, as were two large posters used by the

1.   The Los Angeles Department of Parks and Recreation operated a fully-equipped photo darkroom where I was a member. To join I had to pass a test. To use, I paid a small fee and brought my own printing paper.

conspirators that I designed and made (as called for in the script). I shot still photos as if they were taken during spy surveillance. When Irving Lerner, the editor, needed photos from the Library of Congress, I was on it. He needed the Zapruder film. I ordered it. Someone was needed to read the entire Warren Commission Report. Yes, all twenty-six volumes. I carried the entire set in the backseat of my car for the next several months. I can't recall any of it today; then, I could recite chapter and verse.

I worked with the assistant editor, Ivan Dryer, to assemble the documentary footage used in the film. Ivan introduced me to many of the small businesses that provided services for film producers: titling services, edge coding, optical effects, quick duplicates, negative cutting. Today, due to the digital revolution, all these businesses have gone the way of the buggy whip industry.

I had one other skill that was important in the days before cell phones. I could remember telephone numbers as long as I needed them. How many? Thirty or more. I had a mnemonic trick for remembering. The moment a production was over and I would never need them again, the phone numbers were scrubbed from memory.

I was made a location manager, which meant I negotiated location agreements and went downtown and paid for filming permits. I didn't know LA yet, but with a Thomas Guide² I took on location scouting.

Once principal photography began, I was made assistant to Harry Caplan, the DGA production manager. Unflappable, Harry was always on the move taking care of some important matter. He had credits going back to the early 1930s with the Marx brothers. He had been Marlon Brando's assistant director on the film *One-Eyed Jacks*. I encouraged him to tell me what the production was like . . . and he did. He had deep Hollywood connections.

The director of *Executive Action* was David Miller, who had directed the iconic World War II film *Flying Tigers* with John Wayne. As a WWII film fan, I couldn't believe my luck. *Flying Tigers*!!! Well, it hadn't been my favorite WWII film. Can you love a genre and the title of the film, and think the movie was only, okay? David Miller had numerous credits.

---

2.   Map books of Los Angeles, extremely valuable.

While driving him to check out locations, he told me he would like to be remembered for *Lonely Are the Brave* with Kirk Douglas.

With actors the ilk of Burt Lancaster, Will Geer, and Robert Ryan, David Miller let them deliver their lines with little or no direction. These old pros were perfect on the first take. Two takes happened occasionally. If there needed to be third take, the cause was not these actors. Burt Lancaster, at sixty years old, was in phenomenal physical shape. On the set, if there wasn't a dressing room available, he'd strip down to his tighty-whitey briefs and get into his wardrobe. I overheard Lancaster tell David Miller at one of the first sessions that he wanted to do the film without makeup.

At a production meeting, Harry Caplan made me production manager on a second unit shoot. On the way out of the meeting Gary Horowitz, one of the producers pulled me aside. "Don't let the cameraman go into overtime." Gary was talking about the cinematographer, Allen Daviau. "It's only two shots," Gary insisted.

The second unit crew consisted of Irving Lerner as director; Allen Daviau,[3] the second unit DP; Mack the gaffer with his own lighting equipment truck; the actor Ed Lauter, with his wardrobe; and me as driver, caterer, and everything else. I was getting paid $150 a week but always carried about $400 dollars in petty cash for meals and location fees. I was the person the production and personal assistants came to for gas money.

As far as Allen Daviau was concerned, the production company had not provided him with their best production manager by sending me. We spent several days location scouting and my inexperience probably became apparent. Several times he referred to the "Peter Principle," implying that I had been promoted to the highest level of my incompetence. He was right. I was a cheap option for the producers. Daviau didn't know I was living a master class in filmmaking and getting $150 a week plus gas. I ignored his crap. I didn't know he would be famous one day and win an Academy Award. I thought of him as grandiloquently pretentious.

Ed Lauter, the actor, and I were filmset buddies. A "filmset buddy" is a friendly face you become acquainted with, chat with to pass time, and

3.   Allen Daviau, director of photography on Steven Spielberg's *ET* and *Empire of the Sun*.

if the company is decent you catch up the next time you find yourself with a minute on the set. Ed was an experienced pro. He often played the cop, or sergeant, who had a line or two with the lead in a TV series. We were discussing the idea of "making it" when he related that when he was studying acting in New York, his idea of success was having his name on one of the posters for a Broadway play.

Our second unit location was the Port of Los Angeles. Our assignment was to get the aforementioned two shots of a fictional assassin boarding a merchant vessel. I put on gloves and started dragging out lights, cables, and C-stands with the gaffer. Then we did nothing. Irving asked, "What's happening?"

"I can't light until it's dark," Daviau carped. I found a deli nearby and ordered dinner. It was May. It wouldn't be dark enough to shoot until after 8:30 p.m. I advised Irving about Gary Horowitz's request about not going into overtime. Irving waved his hand, forget about it. If Irving didn't care, I wasn't going to, either. I was only an honorary assistant PM.

Irving Lerner and I had time to talk. He was this show's editor, but he was also a director. Irving adapted one of my favorite novels to film, James T. Farrell's *Studs Lonigan* (1960). He didn't adapt the massive work but selected one of the novel's threads. I'd seen the film years before and remembered it fairly well. I saw the compromise Irving had to make and thought it worked. The film was shot in black and white and had a stark neorealistic look. Irving had cast professional character actors in all the speaking parts. Two actors were at the beginning of their careers, Jack Nicholson (*Easy Rider, Chinatown*) and Frank Gorshin (the Riddler in the *Batman* series, 1966–67).

Irving told me he had shot most of *Studs Lonigan* MOS,[4] a term meaning the scenes were shot without sound. The schedule for the entire film was seven long days. Two days were with the actors on a soundstage. Irving claimed his shooting ratio, meaning the amount of film shot to the footage actually used in the finished production, was about 1.5 to 1. This meant that one-and-a-half minutes of film was shot to every minute of final-cut screen time. Perhaps that was bullshit from an old pro to an amateur, but it could be done. It would require blocking actors as if you

---

4. A German director in the 1930s asked for a scene to be shot without sound, "mit out sound." The cheeky assistant cameraman wrote MOS on the slate.

were doing live television. Every shot had to be planned with exacting care. *Executive Action*, a film being shot efficiently with establishing shots and coverage, had a ratio of six minutes of film shot to one minute of screen time, 6 to 1.

At dusk, Daviau started to set lights. The production needed a wide establishing shot showing the ship and the dock and a medium shot, where the actor's face revealed that he was one of the assassins.

Lighting took three hours with Mack the gaffer, Daviau and me dragging cables, and putting up banks of lights for the shot. He put lights on a warehouse more than fifty yards away, testing and moving lights, then more testing and moving lights. We had walkie-talkies but they didn't speed anything up.

Mack the gaffer pleaded, "It's lit."

Daviau would not be rushed. Ed Lauter kicked back. He was no longer on overtime; he was into "golden time."

At last, we began a rehearsal. Daviau went into a kind of trancelike concentration as he watched Ed go through his blocking. That led to more tweaking with the lights. Then another trance before he turned to Irving Lerner and said he was ready to roll camera. The wide shot was a work of art.

For the second shot, all Ed Lauter had to do was walk up the gangplank and disappear into the ship. I thought we had already lit for that, but Daviau took another hour painting a gorgeous picture with lights and filters. By then, Irving Lerner had fallen asleep. When it was time to shoot, I had the nerve to give Ed a direction. I told him to adjust his sea bag when starting to climb the gangplank. Ed complied. I called, "Action." Daviau shot a second take with no action on the sea bag.

At the dailies the following evening I received kudos from the producers for bringing in the fantastic shots. I can't deny I was pleased with the compliments, but I also felt abused by the exhausting experience.

I ran into Ed Lauter at the filming location several days later where Burt Lancaster was also working. The main dining room in a Mexican restaurant had been converted into the craft services area. I was asked by several extras to have their pictures taken with Burt Lancaster. Burt pleasantly complied. When I finished with the extras, Ed Lauter approached, wanting to know about the rushes from the Los Angeles Harbor. I told him about the kudos from the producers. "All that work for the shot of you climbing the gangplank was worth it. You looked appropriately sinister," I said.

Burt Lancaster overheard my remarks. "How was the old man?" He was speaking directly to me.

"Sir . . ." I stuttered. "I . . . I saw the scene in the mansion . . . with you and Robert Ryan . . . in the garden. It was beautifully shot." With that, Burt Lancaster nodded as if I only confirmed what he already knew, and turned away.

There was no resting on success; one day a hero, the next, the scapegoat. Harry Caplan rented three "cherry pickers," special vehicles with boom arms and risers with a basket at the end, the kind the electric company uses to work on power lines. My job was to get those cherry pickers to the location in Palmdale, California, thirty miles away. I was told the cherry pickers could travel at twenty-five miles an hour on the highway. If we left at 5:00 a.m., we should be there easily by 6:00 a.m. The call time in Palmdale was 8:00 a.m. Planning for contingencies, Harry figured three hours to go thirty miles was reasonable.

Then came the snag. For a good five miles the drive on Interstate 5 (the Grapevine) has a 6%+ uphill grade! The three cherry pickers slowed to five miles an hour. Even on flat stretches of road, they could only manage 16 MPH at best, but 12 MPH on average, and there were more uphill portions ahead. I drove ahead to inform the crew that we would arrive about twenty to thirty minutes late for crew call. In a business where if you arrive fifteen minutes early, you're on time. But, if you arrive at call time, you're late. It's a crappy feeling having the entire crew standing idle, staring at you.

"Cherry pickers are just up the road," David Miller, the director, screamed at me. "They'll be here any minute!"

One of the actors had asked David Miller what was causing the delay. When David said they were waiting for the cherry pickers coming from Los Angeles, the actor spouted, "There are cherry pickers up the road about five miles. I saw the signs as I drove here."

While I waited, humiliated, the production assistant sent to investigate the cherry pickers returned with news. The actor was technically correct, there were cherry pickers, if you were looking for laborers to harvest cherries.

"It's cherry season," I mumbled impishly. David Miller glared at me.

Harry got me off the hook. "Nobody died," he shrugged. "Let's shoot." Our cherry pickers had arrived. The big yellow creatures came lumbering toward us from a quarter of a mile away.

To my surprise, several days after the show wrapped, Allen Daviau called and invited me to lunch. What had changed? He tried to impress me with his gastronomic appreciation of fine cuisine. We never worked together again but occasionally ran into each other at FotoKem Lab. What I learned from Daviau was this: if you're making a feature film, it damn well better look like one. Your work represents you: make it memorable.

I received my first screen credit as "Location Manager" on *Executive Action*. That didn't mean much to the industry folks in Hollywood, but then, I had a whole new set of contacts.

In rural Oaxaca, Mexico, when I took photos of the village women, they would react by pretending they were plucking something from the air with their fingers while making a quick sucking sound with their mouth. They believed I had sucked up a bit of their essence and was taking it far away. They were correct.

5

MONITOS

After *Executive Action* wrapped production, I was hired at Wakeford/ Orloff to work on TV commercials. The job came with an attractive benefit: it paid well. That was fine as long as I didn't question the unseemliness of what the work entails. In TV commercials nothing is sacred. The producers I met were smart, well-educated people who understood television's power to appeal to insecurities, fears, and lust, and they used it to sell deodorant, dog food, automobiles, and political candidates. Did I want to become like these clever, cynical producers? I didn't. For that reason, I choose to make medical, scientific, and education films instead.

Having worked on *Executive Action* for five months, I managed to save about $2,000. Judy and I put $500 in the bank, and with $1,500 we set off to do a documentary film in Mexico. I had become attracted by the work of two Mexican folk artists who made delightful fired clay figures. I wanted to see how these artists worked.

Judy and I flew to Mexico City and visited with an uncle I met once in San Antonio when I was in high school. According to my mother, Martin Elizondo (not his real name) was her cousin from her father's first marriage. A retired medical doctor, Martin had recently separated from his much younger wife. Thus, a man in his sixties had a nine-year-old son, Bruno, and fifteen-year-old daughter, Amelia. They lived on a very pleasant street near the Zona Rosa neighborhood. One of his maids brought freshly made corn tortillas to the dinner table for each meal. We spent two days getting to know our cousins. They were like middle-class kids in the United States: smart, chatty, fun to be with.

From Mexico City we took the train to the city of Oaxaca. We spent most of our time fixed on the spectacular, and at times alarming, mountainous landscape.

We stayed at a small hotel near the center of town and caught the bus to local villages to meet Teodora Blanco and Josefina Aguilar, the two artists whose work I liked.

Teodora was my first choice, but she was working on a commission and had guests from the United Nations. I loved her whimsical figures. Our problem was her village was quite far and there was only one bus per day. Perhaps in the future. I also liked Josefina Aguilar's little men and women. Each figure had its own quirky personality. I commissioned her to make a wedding set: musicians, wedding party, priest, altar boys, and guests. I paid her additionally to allow me to film the process. She said it would take five days, and that's what it took. Judy shot stills and recorded sound as I filmed. Every shot had to advance the story visually. I wanted to capture the transformation of shapeless clay into something, if not art, at least masterful craftsmanship. At the same time, I wanted to give the viewer a glimpse of the world of the Aguilar family.

Here was my Irving Lerner challenge. I had to make a film in Mexico with what I was allowed legally to bring into the country: a 16 mm camera and ten 100-foot rolls of film. That was approximately twenty-seven minutes of film. I owned a hand-wind Bolex with an exterior viewfinder and three lenses (16 mm, 25 mm, and 50 mm). All focus had to be estimated with a depth-of field calculation. I shot Kodak Ektachrome reversal stock (7252 ECO) and used a Weston Ranger 9 light meter for exposures. To record sound, I brought a Sony cassette recorder and the little mic that came with it.

Special film moments don't just happen. To keep shots from looking staged and artificial, I had to wait. Fortunately, the family became accustomed to our presence. I shot handheld and continuously checked focus and exposure anticipating the next shot, and a couple of times rolled film until I knew I had that sequence covered. That approach made for engaging shots but ate up film footage. At that rate I would go through the ten rolls of film too fast. I had to allot enough film for the next four days. I gave myself a quota, two 100-foot rolls per day. That's when the process became especially hard. Every shot had to advance the narrative, while everywhere around me there were glorious panoramas, spectacular sunsets, and an adorable baby donkey in a cornfield with ribbons braided in its mane. We left Oaxaca with everything we hoped we could accomplish.

Did I have qualms about appropriation, and exploitation? I did. Did I understand the implications of what I had done? I didn't want to hurt the family. If the film was any good, it might bring some attention to their craftmanship, but I had no idea if anything we shot and documented was usable.

Back in Los Angeles, I processed the motion picture film and the stills. Everything looked good. Judy had done an excellent job with still photography and sound, and I did a passable job as a cameraman. We had a film, and more.

I did the first assembly on the Craig editing device I'd had since San Antonio. I then rented an editing room with a Moviola in Hollywood. My story was there in the footage. The focus was a little iffy in one shot, but it worked in the context of the whole, which was the taking of a chunk of clay, making an entire wedding set, firing it, and painting it. The film felt natural and un-staged.

I hired Scott Dailey to create a guitar score for the film and a professional actress to do the narration. The sound effects were done at Audio Effects, a sound studio in Hollywood. Business must have been slow because the mixers were really glad to see me. They took my cassette recording and created the ambient tracks. Then they matched the action on the screen with sound effects they created, as in the buzz of a fly, or footsteps. It made the action on the screen feel immediate and real.

Judy and I created an entire educational package: a children's book, a slideshow, a teacher's guide, and the film. We assembled a prototype and took it to distributors and learned the cold, horrible truth: companies that sell books are not the same as the companies that package curriculum, and they do not distribute films. Only film distributors distribute films.

I took the edited film to FilmFair Communications and they took it on the spot. They offered me $3,200 as an advance against royalties, and gave me $5,200 to go back to Oaxaca and make another film. I wasn't doing this for the money. I was lucky to have done better than break even.

Even by 1973 standards, I was making films incredibly cheaply. I could have haggled for more money, but my eleven-minute film, *Monitos*, got a full page with photos in the classy, expensively printed FilmFair educational film catalog. That was great publicity for a filmmaker.

FilmFair Communications did the final lab work for *Monitos* at Technicolor Lab. I felt intimidated. I was having the lab work for my first film done in the same rooms as major motion pictures.

Inexpensive filmmaking came to an end in the middle 1970s when two Dallas financiers, the Hunt Brothers, tried to corner the silver market. The price for 400 feet of 16 mm Kodak film, which was $16 in 1973, suddenly shot up to $46. The lab costs for processing and work prints went up accordingly. Eventually, the price of silver came down, but the price of film never did. I considered it economic censorship.

There are no rules in filmmaking. Only sins.
And the cardinal sin is dullness.
—Frank Capra

6

. . . . AND THE EARTH
DID NOT DEVOUR HIM

My father held Dr. Américo Paredes, renowned historian, folklorist, and musician, in high regard. I don't know if my father ever read anything Dr. Paredes wrote. In 1974, dad was president of the Southwest Gem and Mineral Society and hosted an event where Dr. Paredes lectured. Dad saved a news clipping that said Paredes wrote for Pacific *Stars and Stripes* during World War II. The lecture and whatever word-of-mouth stories existed about Américo Paredes were what Dad knew, and that was enough.

Unrelated to the esteem my father had for Dr. Paredes, I made an appointment to pitch the professor an idea of a documentary about Mexican corridos. My idea was to weave the narrative from his book, *With a Pistol in His Hand,* with actors, and intersperse the stories with some of the best traditional musicians performing the verses to *El Corrido de Gregorio Cortez*. He listened patiently, thought the idea was too flashy, and dismissed me. Other than my father, the only person whose respect I would have liked to have had was Américo Paredes's. I never regretted approaching him to adapt his book; at least I'd given the idea a shot.

I met Dr. Tomás Rivera that same year while working as a production manager for Moctesuma Esparza on a McGraw-Hill documentary. This was many years before Moctesuma produced *Cisco Kid* (1994) *and Selena* (1998). Tomás Rivera had been recommended as a possible profile subject. He'd recently won the first Quinto Sol Award for his novel . . . *and the earth did not devour him*. He was associate dean and an English professor at the University of Texas, San Antonio. A robust, amiable man, he waved us into his office. I had not read his novel, but Tomás didn't make a big deal about it. He didn't have that glow of self-importance writers sometimes have when praised for their work. He was not selected as a subject for the documentary. However, Tomás's warmth left an impression on me. I liked him immensely.

Later that year while attending a conference in San Francisco, I had lunch with artist and good friend, Carmen Lomas Garza, a Texas transplant like myself. We dropped by the Galeria de la Raza, a gallery and bookstore in the Mission District. I purchased two books that day, *Bless Me, Ultima* by Rudolfo Anaya, and . . . *and the earth did not devour him* by Tomás Rivera. The books sat on my desk for several months.

I'd been busy. Dan Bessie, who owned Learning Garden, the educational film production company I mentioned previously, turned over producing to me. We had a contract to produce patient counseling medical films for a client. Work can become insanely intense at a production company, but basics like film processing and other steps simply take time and are out of a producer's hands. It was during one of those down moments that I picked up Tomás Rivera's . . . *and the earth did not devour him*. I began to read and didn't stop until I finished. The language, the people, the locales, the situations were immediately familiar. I knew that Bartolo Ortiz, the poet/musician character in the book, was a real person. I grew up in Westside San Antonio. My family didn't do migrant work, but my grandfather was a vegetable peddler, and I grew up around the city's wholesale produce market. Our neighbors, the Montez family, went to the *piscas* /harvests every year. We were poor; our Montez neighbors were poorer.

The eighty-seven-page novella had a powerful effect on me. Tomás had made literature from his own experiences as a migrant worker. He and I may not have been from the same neighborhood, but we read the same newspapers, heard the same folk tales, listened to the same music. We were, for the lack of a better word, from the same tribe.

I needed to speak with Tomás. I stared at the phone. I knew where he worked. I called UTSA and asked to speak to Dr. Tomás Rivera. I was transferred to the English Department, transferred again to his office, and finally transferred to his phone. A cheerful bass voice answered, "Hello."

I told Tomás who I was and that we'd met. I told him I thought his book was poetic and profound. I told him I wanted to make it into a movie.

I heard a chuckle. I have no idea what he thought of this near-stranger wanting to make his book into a film. He didn't say "no," nor did he hang up on me. I took that as an opening. I repeated my request and ended with, "Thank you. I'll be in touch."

At that moment in time, I knew I didn't have a clue how one goes about optioning a novel, nor did I have the technical and artistic experience to pull anything like that off. However, it didn't keep me from impetuously believing I could do it. While reading . . . *and the earth did not devour him*, at that moment, at the beginning of my career, I saw the movie I wanted to make. Most choices I would make in the future were aimed at preparing myself to write and direct this film.

7

CURVES IN THE ROAD

I studied acting with several teachers with no intention of performing myself, but to learn to speak to actors. Acting looks easy when Meryl Streep does it. It's not. It takes years of rehearsals and performances before an actor feels comfortable enough with their craft that they can deliver any line, any time, any place, with perfect inflection. Concert musicians play instruments. The actor's instrument is their entire body, and their voice is only one part. The often repeated saying is true: Not all great actors are stars, and not all stars are great actors. It helps to have a gift.

I considered writing to be my strongest skill. I had ideas, but had nothing committed to paper. At an acting workshop at Nosotros, a Latino actors' advocacy group, I met actress Lupe Ontiveros. She had a gift. Lupe was irresistibly likeable. I loved to watch her work. Her honest delivery, her subtle body language and facial expressions could instantly create a bawdy barmaid, a concerned social worker, or a busy mom, which she was. I wrote a one-act play, *Angie*, about three women contending with a sexually harassing housing manager, a comedy. I cast Lupe and two other women in the workshop. Eager to participate, they quickly learned their lines. After several rehearsals, I stopped by the Los Angeles Theater Center and asked the manager if I could stage the one-act play for one night. This was when the theater was in seedy East Hollywood, on Oxford Street off Santa Monica Boulevard. The theater was dark the following week. I must have looked harmless. The manager said, yes. I made phone calls, put out flyers at the Inner City Cultural Center and the Nosotros office.

About thirty people showed up, among them Carmen Zapata, then doyenne of Latino Theater in LA. The following morning Carmen showed up at the Learning Garden office and invited me to adapt a popular Mexican play, *Los Desarraigados*, into English. There was no money in it at the moment, but I would get credit in the program and $100 at the end. Such a deal! I said, yes.

I became an integral part of the staging of *Los Desarraigados/ Uprooted*, as part of Mark Taper's 1977 Ford Theatre series. Besides translating the play, I shot publicity stills, sat in on all rehearsals, and produced a slideshow that opened the performance. As translator, I also served as Chicano cultural consultant. Carmen Zapata was a New York–trained actress. I never learned what nation made her Latina. She had performed in New York under the name Margaret Cameron. Margarita Galban, the director, was Cuban, and Estela "Piqui" Scarlata, the set designer, was from Argentina. All three were talented professionals suited to staging Federico García Lorca, Eugene O'Neill, or Samuel Beckett. However, their assumptions about Mexican American culture were way off. I'll leave it at that. A *pocho*-English melodrama set in East Los Angeles needed to be carefully crafted. *Los Desarraigados* was written for a Mexican audience and had a clear anti-American bias. Carmen, Margarita, and Piqui saw nothing wrong with that. I argued and persuaded Carmen that Mexican Americans are not necessarily recent immigrants and are decidedly not anti-American. They do resent being treated as second-class citizens in a place where they have roots. That was the important distinction. I reshaped the events and dialogue to reflect conflicts that Mexican Americans could relate to, as in discrimination in the workplace and abusive treatment by police.

The central character of *Los Desarraigados/Uprooted* was the father who is fired from his job after being falsely accused of drug possession. He had more lines than the mother. Carmen, who was playing the mother, ordered me to rewrite the dialogues so that she would have more lines. She insisted Mexican culture was matriarchal, therefore justified. I disagreed, argued otherwise, and lost.

I made as many changes as I thought retained the author's intent. Carmen counted the lines, and still had fewer lines than the father. Carmen didn't change any of the text; she just took enough of the father's lines until she had more. The play worked. The father still had the weighty scenes in the play. Julio Medina, the actor playing the father, nailed his final scene every night. The audiences enjoyed the play. Ultimately, the kerfuffle didn't make any difference. The playwright, Humberto Robles Arenas, came to a performance and approved the English adaptation.

One evening after the performance, Jose Luis Ruiz, a local producer who I didn't know at the time, was holding court in the lobby of the Ford Theatre. Surrounded by a group of his friends, he criticized my adaptation of *Uprooted* as not being "barrio enough." His smile reminded me of an ad for dentures. He opined that the teenage kid in the play should be more like the Fonzie Fonzarelli character in the TV series *Happy Days*. Normally, I wouldn't remember a ridiculous comment like that, since I had nothing to do with the casting or direction of *Uprooted*. I had a great time doing the play and was damn lucky to be part of it. Regrettably, this guy would keep reappearing in my life.

There were many circles of influence in LA. There were the clichéd Olvera Street Mexicans on call as movie extras and for party entertainment. There were the politicos, each with smaller and larger circles of influence. There were the corporate Hispanic minority types, the kind who funded Carmen Zapata's Bilingual Foundation, her theater company.

In regard to me, there were the local Chicano filmmakers: Moctesuma Esparza, Jesús Treviño, and Jose Luis Ruiz, all at the beginning of their careers and linked by a defining moment: the events of August 29, 1970, the Chicano Moratorium March. Tens of thousands of people marched peacefully to memorialize the disproportionate number of deaths of Mexican American soldiers in the Vietnam War. What happened that day would leave an indelible mark on the psyche of Los Angeles. Judy, my future wife, was present and saw how the peaceful demonstration was violently crushed when the police fired noxious tear gas into the crowd. Some of the Los Angeles Chicano filmmakers were there with cameras. Three people were killed by the police, including the famed Chicano journalist, Ruben Salazar.

Even though I was 1,500 miles away, still living in San Antonio, I was affected by that day; perhaps not in the same way as the LA filmmakers. Ruben Salazar's articles on the systemic discrimination against Mexicans, the treatment of prisoners in El Paso jails, the Tlatelolco Massacre had been validating touchstones. He expressed in his reporting what I saw in the world around me. I had a lot in common ideologically with the LA filmmakers. Still, I was from San Antonio, not East LA.

About a year after the successful production of *Uprooted*, Carmen Zapata called me and wanted to meet at a restaurant in West Los Angeles. I was greeted by C. Bernard Jackson, the director of the Inner City Cultural Center, and Michael Dewell, who represented himself as Carmen's "agent." As we waited for Carmen to make her entrance, Dewell made a snotty comment he attributed to a famous theater legend, "Never work with amateurs." Somehow, I got the uneasy feeling Dewell was referring to me.

When Carmen arrived, it became clear that my suspicion was accurate. Carmen wanted me to sign away any claim to the translator's credit of *Uprooted*. Michael Dewell and C. Bernard Jackson were there as witnesses for my signing of a release of claim to translator credit. I had utmost respect for Jackson, but he sat there sheepishly without saying a word. What Carmen failed to disclose was that she had received a grant from the California Arts Council to perform *Uprooted* in cities across the state. With the signed and witnessed document, she became the sole translator and earned the substantial translator's fee. Carmen was true to her word. She had said up front I'd get $100. Lesson learned. That's life in Hollywood. Moving on.

8

MARKET DAY

In 1974, Judy and I traveled to Mexico to make our second film for FilmFair Communications. This time we decided to drive to Oaxaca. We loaded up my new 1974 Dodge delivery van and drove to San Antonio, Texas, for our first stop.

There were several things I wanted to do to in San Antonio. I wanted to follow up with eighty-year-old Mr. Jose Garza, a *curandero* and supplier of herbal teas and remedies. I had interviewed him the previous year and hoped to spend several hours with him again. I wanted to visit my parents, as well. However, the main reason I needed to swing by San Antonio was because my friend, Alberto Mijangos, had a position with the Mexican consulate. The last time I was in San Antonio I told Alberto about filming in Mexico. He offered to help if I needed it with a filming permit.

I'd known Alberto since 1969, a year after HemisFair, a world's fair for half the world. He was director of the Mexican-American Cultural Exchange Institute, housed in a building used the previous year as Mexico's pavilion. We became friends, partied, talked about art, Texas/Tejano culture, drank too much tequila, and ate cans of *anguilas*, tiny baby eels, on crackers. They were incredibly good. I tried to buy some at the local upscale market in Los Angeles. They were in a locked case and sold for over $70 dollars for a tiny can. They were more expensive than caviar. In Alberto's kitchen, drinking tequila, we must have gone through a case.

I had heard he had separated from his wife. I called him the week before we left Los Angeles and asked about the filming permit he'd offered. He said he didn't foresee a problem. Once we were in San Antonio, he was hard to get hold of and didn't return calls. We were only in San Antonio for forty-eight hours. I called him late at night and finally got him on the phone. He asked me to come by the consulate the following afternoon, which I did, only to find he had left for the day. That was a problem because Judy and I were leaving for Oaxaca in the morning. I persisted, and he finally responded that I should drop by his apartment. He lived at the Aurora Apartments near McCullough, across from Crockett Park. We stopped by but he did not answer his door or his phone. Shit!

I had planned to make a stop that day to see Jose Garza, the *curandero*. I was now pressed for time. It irritated me that Mijangos was being evasive. I stopped trying to chase him and headed to visit Mr. Garza's *botanica* on Poplar and Zarzamora Streets. I don't know why, but a visit to his shop was always rewarding.

Housed in a sagging wooden 1890s commercial storefront with apartments upstairs, the shop was tiny. I pushed open the weathered screen door and a small bell jingled. Mr. Garza stepped out from the back room and greeted us. He remembered me, of course. This was Judy's first visit to a *botanica*.

Only three or four customers could fit in the tiny shop. The room always held an instant aromatic surprise, pleasing and memorably distinct. Bundles of fresh herbs hung on the walls. A faded artwork featured an avenging angel wielding a sword striking down the devil. In the corner, overlooking the room, was a small altar to St. Anthony of Padua holding the infant Jesus. Under the counter a cabinet with many narrow drawers held his ingredients. The *botanica* had become frozen in time. Objects in his glass display case had not changed in the several years I'd visited the shop. Except for the fresh herbs, the only thing different in the room was a green and yellow caterpillar poised on top of the gumball dispenser munching on a twig of fresh herb. It raised its head as I approached, then returned to eating.

Suddenly, I felt foolish. I had forgotten to bring the photos my brother Rene had taken of Mr. Garza the previous year. I don't believe in ghosts, Santa Claus, or God. I do believe teas and herbs have powers to stimulate or soothe. Mr. Garza must have had a clientele for his ingredients because he managed to stay in business all these years. As an excuse for my visit, I told him where we were going, what we were doing, and asked if he could make an amulet for our trip.

The gentle Mr. Garza took several eight-inch square sheets of red tissue paper, aligned them as one and placed them on the counter. He reached into one of the cabinet drawers and retrieved a small lodestone and placed it in the center of the red papers. Into that magnetic field he added iron filings, which formed two coronas. He added a minuscule link from a gold chain, a red mountain laurel seed, and clippings of several herbs. He added what looked like a miniature scapular and a tiny religious medal of Mary. He paused to say prayers, then added a sprinkling of quartz crystals, tiny garnets, and a pinch of earth. He prayed again, then folded the red tissue papers over the lodestone and its magnetic mass in the center. He ended with a neat two-inch square pillow, which he tied deftly with red string. There was a kind of Japanese ritual perfection about the process and result. He slid the red amulet into an appropriately sized envelope along with printed devotionals to various saints. He solemnly prayed again and handed the closed envelope to me. I had the impression I wasn't supposed to open it.

I thanked Mr. Garza and paid him. Back in my van I put the envelope with the amulet in the glove compartment next to my travel clock and forgot about it.

Alberto finally answered the phone at 9:30 p.m. Yes, he was home. Come on by.

We went up to his place and knocked. A moment later, Alberto answered the door in his underwear. A woman, a Latina, was there with him. She scurried to her feet, clearly peeved, "That's rude, insisting on dropping by." She then melted into the background and sulked.

Alberto presented me with a legal-size envelope. I opened it. The letter on consulate stationery appeared to say I was who was, and I was authorized to bring 3,000 feet of film into Mexico. He wouldn't take any money.

How was I to know his offer to help with a filming permit had been a hollow diplomatic courtesy? Alberto was drunk and a little pissed. "I know you, and I know your limitations," he said. "Do you think you are going to discover Mexico? What do you know about Mexico? You barely speak Spanish."

"You offered. You said it would be no problem. Alberto, thank you. I'm sorry to interrupt your evening." Judy and I backed out as quickly as we could.

The next morning, we were off. Fortunately, Alberto's paper got us through the border and checkpoints. Alberto was right in his alcohol-soaked moment of truth. What did I know about Mexico? Damn Little. What was I doing? I told myself I was doing research to find out who I am. Perhaps I could find a clue in Mexico.

Judy and I had flown the last time we went to Mexico. Seeing the magnificent vistas from the front seat of the Dodge van was a revelation.

We drove to my uncle's house in Mexico City. Our host, Martin Elizondo, greeted us warmly. He was amused we were traveling and sleeping in the van. "The *luna de miel* suite," he named it.

Martin took the document Alberto Mijangos had given me to the appropriate office. When he returned, he handed me the permit. "I got you the permit, but they laughed at the letter from the San Antonio consulate. They said it was a joke. You were lucky the people at the border didn't stop you."

His children, Amelia and Bruno, were preoccupied with school and weren't as much fun as during our last visit. Martin wanted me to meet one of our cousins. This side of the family was very proud to be relatives of Venustiano Carranza, president of Mexico (1915–20), which made me one of them. I was more than a little ambivalent about that. I had aunts who never married because they would have had to marry below their station. Mom married a mestizo, not some highborn aristocrat. As a boy I had experienced my Mexican relatives' disapproval of my swarthy complexion before I experienced it from the gringos.

My mother celebrated her first birthday May 21, 1920, the same day president Carranza was assassinated. By one account, the family was given two weeks to leave the country, in another story they fled for their lives with bullets flying. Of course, both or neither story could be true. The family arrived in the United States by train, as refugees. If her father had money, mom didn't know it. She experienced lean years during her childhood in the United States.

Cousin Amelia accompanied us on the visit to Victoria Ferriño (not her real name), the cousin from my mother's side of the family. A commanding woman in her fifties, she showed us around her grand house designed by her architect son. It was a place for entertaining, with spacious patios and vistas. What impressed Judy and me was the main bathroom done entirely in the most tasteful Talavera tiles we'd ever seen. Even the sink, the tub, and the toilet repeated the room's Talavera patterns.

Victoria was a photographer of some note, and her book of photos lay on a side table large enough to allow the book to lay open.

She nodded to Judy and me, and turned to Amelia. "Should I speak in front of your cousins?"

Amelia, nodded, unsure what was happening.

Victoria informed us that Amelia had given birth only weeks before, and had given up the child to the boy's family. Victoria was furious. "A mother does not give up a child!" she said, harshly. Amelia began to weep. Judy and I didn't want to be there. We were embarrassed for the humiliated girl.

When Victoria finished berating poor Amelia, she then turned to me and wanted to know what I did. I fumbled my way through the conversation, telling her about the film I made the previous year about folk artists in Oaxaca.

"Artists in Oaxaca," Victoria became animated. She named several artists.

"No, I don't know them."

"They're fine artists." She went on that one of them had shows at the Chicago Art Institute, and the Whitney Museum and was, "very famous."

"I made a film about a folk artist. They're Zapotecs still plowing the fields with oxen, and planting corn, beans, and squash."

"Why would you make a film about the Indians?" she asked derisively.

Knowing Victoria also spoke English, I stopped fumbling. "I am fascinated with their art, and perhaps because I am part indigenous, too."

From here on the conversation continued in English. She turned to Judy, "What do you do?"

"I'm an elementary school teacher," Judy replied.

"You both work. How many servants do you have?"

"We can't afford servants," Judy said.

"None? None at all?" We shook our heads.

"Here, we must have servants; otherwise, the poor would starve."

Judy and I exchanged a look. Earlier, Victoria had screamed at the maid for taking so long to bring coffee. We were eager to clear out of her lovely house.

Before we left Mexico City, I asked Martin to clarify my relationship to the descendants of the assassinated, aristocratic president. It turned out I was related by marriage, not DNA. I felt relieved.

While the drive to Mexico City had been a revelation, the drive to Oaxaca was spectacular and more than a little scary. The steep mountains and distant valleys brought to mind Voltaire's *Candide*. Candide finds himself in a magnificent exotic land where toy balls are made of gold. He rests from his travels, and when he departs, he carries away as many golden balls his pack animals can carry. As he descends the treacherous mountains, he watches the golden orbs spill away. These mountains in Oaxaca could do just that. We drove by many roadside altars, shrines to tragic accidents.

The indigenous people of Oaxaca are diminutive. Judy is five feet tall and was taller than the average woman.

I wanted to make a film portrait of one day at an itinerant market in Oaxaca. Judy and I visited market days in different villages. The market day in each village took on its own character. We introduced ourselves to the venders and asked if we could come back and film them working.

I envisioned an empty plaza and quiet streets. The venders would arrive by bus, truck, or with loaded donkeys. They would unpack and set up their stalls, transforming the plaza into a noisy crowded marketplace. At the end of the day the market would wind down, the plaza and streets once again returning to quiet.

The town I chose was Ocotlán, about thirty minutes from the city of Oaxaca. I made a checklist of shots that would best describe certain parts of the day. I needed to show the different shopping zones: live animals, fruits and vegetables, the corn area, earthenware, woven goods (baskets and mats), clothing. I also wanted to show related activities, people having a meal, socializing. A woman in modest business attire sat at a small table with a manual typewriter. She wrote letters, filled out forms for clients, and provided the addressed envelope and stamp.

I had a conversation with an older rope maker, one of the less influential venders among the younger more aggressive rope sellers. My rope maker was a chatty man. He was hoping to make a big sale and invited us to visit his house where he would show us how he made rope. The next morning, we drove there and met his wife and granddaughter.

His wife, a tiny woman, wore the traditional attire, an apron and the black-and-white rebozo. Even though the rope maker's Zapotec wife spoke little Spanish, and Judy was just learning Spanish, somehow, they managed to communicate quite well. The rope-maker couple were proud of the two-room cinder-block house with a corrugated tin roof their son had built for them. The front door was still a work in progress. Chickens and a young turkey losing its baby fuzz pecked around the enclosed yard.

I filmed the rope maker taking strands of sisal and spinning them into rope, I filmed him leaving for the market. I didn't follow him that day because he was going to a different town. I paid him five dollars and said I would come by in the morning and we would follow him to Ocotlán. I envisioned the rope maker as a framing device: going to market, working at the market, and returning home. We would see him three times to connect the viewer to a real person.

When we arrived the next morning, the rope maker's wife tearfully informed us in sign and mime that her husband had used the money to go on a bender. When would he be well? I asked. In her limited Spanish she said, five days.

I doubled down on capturing *verité* portraits of the venders and customers, taking into account the time of day and location in the market. I watched for gestures or reactions that defined the moment, as in the instant when a salesman closed a deal.

We did okay. I'd lost my rope maker but fulfilled the challenge. Judy shot stills and recorded ambient tracks. I'd saved a roll of film just in case my rope maker sobered up. We went back to his house. He was still incapacitated. I felt badly for the wife. I gave her the money I would have given to her husband.

On the way back to town, I saw the movie house was showing a film titled *De Sangre Chicana*. By some unbelievable coincidence, my first cousin, Bonnie Cortez, from San Antonio, starred in that film. Bonnie is a talented musician with a beautiful, trained singing voice. She graduated from the University of Texas and, as far as I knew, was a high school music teacher. What I didn't know was that Bonnie had become a popular singer at the fancier clubs on San Antonio's Riverwalk. I had learned from my parents that a Mexican movie company had come to San Antonio and she had been cast in the female lead. The film was showing right there in Oaxaca that night.

We parked the van in a well-lit intersection with shops and people nearby. The shopkeepers had seen us and we'd shopped in their stores. We had never been away from the van without our equipment and film before. We were taking a chance. We would only be gone for an hour and a half. We had to see the film.

In the theater, a decent crowd of petite *oaxaqueños* filled the seats. We were given a few curious looks, but once the film began, the audience was into the sentimental story.

How to describe the film? It's about a family in San Antonio, Texas. The oldest son is a medical student by day and secretly a masked wrestler by night. The love interest is this sweet girl, Bonnie, my cousin. The family is in financial trouble and the wrestler son must work for a living, sacrificing his dream of becoming a doctor. The story also takes place in an upstairs-downstairs world of servants and minor gentry, a cultural phenomenon virtually nonexistent in Texas. The family had a gossipy maid, who flirted with the local cop in the kitchen. North Americans were portrayed as comical stereotypes, the kind of people who add an "o" at the end of a word to make it "Spanish." Production values were minimal. Most of the film was dubbed. Bonnie did not sing. I doubted an English version would ever be made. As the film ended and credits rolled, there wasn't a dry eye in the house. The film had delivered its audience.

The intersection where we had parked our van was deserted, the shops closed and no one was on the streets. As we approached the van, I saw the driver's side window was open. Panic. I hadn't left the window open. I ran to the door. There was a man in my van. I opened the door and climbed in with no idea what I was going to do. I grabbed the man by the arm and shouted "*Ratero, Ratero.*" The man reached for a knife and I backed away. He opened the passenger side door and fled, disappearing into the darkness.

Judy was upset with me. Yes, I could have gotten hurt. I was okay. Our van had been searched. Every bag had been opened, yet everything was there. My camera and tape recorder were safe. He had not opened the film cans.

A knock on the passenger side window startled me. Outside a short Oaxacan man dressed in a white peasant shirt and trousers and wearing huaraches stared at me. I rolled down the window. He handed me the amulet Mr. Jose Garza had made for me. The envelope had been opened, but the amulet was intact and undamaged.

When we did a complete inventory of the van, the only thing missing was our travel clock. We took it as a sign. Our time in Oaxaca was up.

I thought about Alberto Mijangos's admonition. Did I discover Mexico? What was I trying to do? I showed decent, attractive people going about their lives. That they had different customs and priorities was the point.

Back in Los Angeles, I edited an eighteen-minute version I liked, and named it *Tianguis,* the ancient name for market day. This time I didn't use a music score. I created a sound effects score. I didn't try to dub voices, but I did use voices as sound effects to support the visuals.

The FilmFair producer loved the film; with exceptions, naturally, "It has to be twelve minutes long, have narration, and the name has to be in English. What does *Tianguis* mean?"

"Market Place," I said.

"Great. That's the name, *Market Place in Mexico.* Nobody will buy a film if they don't know what it means. Great job, by the way."

9

CUL DE SAC

In 1975, Moctesuma Esparza introduced me to international award-winning actor-director, Alfonso Arau. His critically and commercially successful films in Mexico and Latin America meant little to Hollywood.
Alfonso was looking for a project. He apparently had backing from a coffee millionaire. I don't know what arrangement Moctesuma and Alfonso
had. They decided to make a film together and hired me to ghostwrite
it for Alfonso. This was eighteen years before Alfonso made *Like Water
for Chocolate* (1992). We spent two weeks touring the US-Mexico border from Brownsville, Texas, to San Ysidro, California, to gather material,
locations, and atmosphere for the story Alfonso had in mind.

I confronted a deep flaw in myself during my time traveling
with Alfonso and Moctesuma. I was shamefully ignorant, like most
Americans, about immigration policy and history. That kind of information can be learned. What I wasn't ready to see was the human cost of it
all. We witnessed an Immigration and Naturalization Service (INS) raid
on a business. The INS agents rounded up the workers and forced the
apprehended men to sit in the INS trucks, silent in their humiliation.

A female INS agent scurried around the stacks of boxes like a terrier
running down a rabbit. A man in the warehouse appeared to be having
a seizure; another worker, not detained by INS, wept silently. I shot a
roll of stills during the horrible mess and was spotted by someone who
looked like corporate security. I furtively unloaded my camera and hid
the film in my shoe. I reloaded the camera and shot off as many frames
as I could before Alfonso, Moctesuma, and I were summoned to the

main office. Three lanky men sat drinking coffee. They were seemingly okay with what was taking place in their business, but the photos I was taking, that was a problem. They demanded I hand over the negatives. I refused, at first. When it became clear that they would take my camera, I opened the back and pulled the film out, exposing it. I put the tangle of exposed film on their desk. They didn't believe that was the roll I shot, and they were right. At that moment several INS officers entered the room. Corporate security couldn't search me or put a hand on me with so many witnesses. We excused ourselves and got the hell out of there.

At the San Ysidro border crossing, the chief Border Patrol officer tried to sound evenhanded by making an offensive comparison: "Trash from both sides collects along the fence."

Alfonso called his script-writing construction "ultra-baroque," meaning story elements were like curlicues flowing into more curlicues. Every scene had a beginning that evolved with conflict or interaction, which then connected to the next scene. Within each scene, the visual and narrative elements continued the pattern of detail, and then more detail. Alfonso was a talented filmmaker. I enjoyed his films *Inspector Calzonzin* and *El Aguila Descalza*.

Alfonso was acutely aware of money and social station. He could gauge a person's wealth and motives fairly accurately. He could be genial and socially polished in a Giorgio Armani suit, but when an associate crossed him, I saw how quickly he could draw blood. Those perceptions found their way into the script I was ghostwriting for Alfonso. I learned a lot, as in, I learned Alfonso owed money. He was often just a few steps ahead of creditors. He bragged that when you have a box office hit, all is forgiven. Those were not words I could live by. I was glad when my gig was over and moved on.

However, that wasn't the end for Alfonso and Moctesuma. Their disagreement about money thankfully didn't involve me. Moctesuma had an I'm-the-smartest-guy-in the-room swagger but it wasn't a match for Alfonso's go-for-the-jugular psych warfare. Alfonso fathomed Moctesuma's deepest personal insecurities and used them. Moctesuma sued Alfonso. When that didn't work, the situation became so acrimonious that Moctesuma tried to have Alfonso deported. I was acquainted with Antonio Rodriguez, Alfonso's attorney. He confirmed the rumor that, indeed, Moctesuma tried to have Alfonso deported, and the script I ghostwrote was lost forever in the litigation.

As for the roll of the still photos I shot during the INS raid, I carried the cartridge in my briefcase for a couple of months. I was about to drop off another roll of film at the lab for processing and proof sheets when I paused at the doorway. I didn't want to be reminded of the worker having a seizure or another weeping at the loss of his companions. I yanked the unexposed film from the canister, exposing it to light, and tossed it in the 55-gallon trash barrel for the rejects and failures the lab kept by the door. I wish I could have done the same with my shame.

10

THE FOLIOSCOPE

How did I learn about animation? Actually, I've known from the time I was five years old how individual drawings merge into motion.

In January 1946, my mother, my toddler brother, and I moved in with my paternal grandparents. I didn't know it at the time, but my father was coming home from the war. Mom was preparing for his return. She took me with her to visit a woman friend, Myrna, who lived less than two blocks from my grandfather's place. Her wood frame house was like others on the block, except it needed painting. The wood had turned an ashen gray. The front door opened into a tidy living room with a 1930s-style sofa, a Boston fern, and porcelain tchotchkes. I don't know if I actually saw those things, except they often accompanied the real images I do remember: starched crocheted doilies on the coffee table and floor-model radio console.

Mom was there to have her hair done. Myrna made a big deal of how nice I looked. More than likely, I fidgeted. Before they went into the next room, Myrna placed a curious looking box on the coffee table. It was an animation flipbook machine with a viewing window. There were several complete stories, nothing complicated: a premise, a setup, followed by the payoff. They were black-and-white drawings that today I would associate with Max Fleischer–style cartoons.

The flipbook machine's design was easy to understand. By turning a hand crank, I could make the drawings come to life. I could slow the action, speed it up, stop it, or play it backward. What fascinated me was how one drawing could be rather uninteresting, but when a series of drawings, each slightly different from the preceding one, were seen as a continuous flow, they came alive. It was like magic because, in fact, it was. I may not have known about the persistence of vision, but right then I understood how the art of animation was created. The flipbook machine captivated me long enough to allow Mom to finish her appointment.

The next day I begged Mom to take me back. "Why do you want to go back?"

"I like her."

"You like, Myrna?"

"She's nice. I want to go back."

That afternoon, Mom walked me over to Myrna's just to say, hello. Mom began telling Myrna that I wanted to come back to visit because she was so nice. Before Mom could finish saying as much, I had found the flipbook machine and was reengrossed.

Myrna cracked, "Well, we know what he really wants. Just like a man." I was surprisingly ashamed for all men as much as a five-year-old could be. I'd been found out. I had misrepresented my affections to get what I wanted.

My father came home that night and we soon moved to another neighborhood. If Mom returned to Myrna's, I didn't know. The memory of how the flipbook machine worked has stayed with me for over seventy-five years.

I have looked for years for a flipbook machine like Myrna's. The closest I've found is a Midgette Toy Company Folioscope, though I'm not sure if that was the device. The viewing screening doesn't seem familiar. What does appear memorable is the large Rolodex-style wheel with hundreds of animated drawings. I've seen a picture of a Midgette Toy Company Folioscope online. The case has been painted fire-engine red, perhaps to cover over the badly faded original decorations. There are indentations and marks on top. The Folioscope could be missing parts, perhaps a marquee, or a viewing device.

In 1976, I was supervising live-action sequences on a medical film for Learning Garden, the film production company. Dan Bessie worked on the animated sequences. I watched as he made small adjustments to the drawing of a character on a paper cel, then with a cel between each finger, he deftly flipped through several cels to watch the action. I appreciated that the word, "animation," meant bringing to life.

11

SUNSET BOULEVARD

Dan Bessie, animator-director, started Learning Garden in 1972 as a boutique film production company. When I joined the company in 1974, besides Dan, Mallory Pearce was designing medical and scientific animation. Learning Garden's major client distributed patient counseling films about macular degeneration, cataracts, diabetes, hypertension, STDs, vaginitis, among others. For that last film, I supervised the artful illustrations of vaginas, which received nodding approval from the client and the consulting doctor.

Between 1974 and 1978, Learning Garden made numerous medical films and several longer productions, meaning we were in constant production. By 1978, Dan Bessie had run the company for six years. He had tired of the producing grind. He wanted to close Learning Garden and concentrate on directing. I thought there was a future for Learning Garden, so I purchased the company, incorporated, and moved the office to Sunset Boulevard, across the street from the Screen Actors Guild and Dino's Restaurant.

John Morrill sold me his editing equipment. The antique upright Moviola was the main feature in my office/editing room. At other production companies, the new Steenbeck flatbed editing machines were all the rage. They had Chevy Corvettes; I had a Model T Ford. Considering John Morrill's penchant for perfection, my antique looked great and worked like new. It required less space and was faster, considering the Moviola's only purpose was for assembling the film. The 3 1/4 × 4-inch screen was not for showing clients. We screened films for clients at

FotoKem Lab or at a screening room a block away. Projection rooms were available everywhere in Hollywood and Burbank.

I landed contracts with National Institutes of Health, Infinity Factory, and WNET (New York). Learning Garden clients were listed in *Daily Variety*'s weekly TV production listings.

One of the reasons I chose to proceed with the business was because a twenty-four-year-old African American artist named Bill Davis asked me for a job. He had recently become a father and needed steady work. I took a look at his portfolio and knew I could sell what he could do.

I used the company earnings to produce two award-winning educational films using the talents of my wife Judy (writer), Dan Bessie, Mallory Pearce, and Bill Davis. *Astronauts and Jellybeans*, narrated by Brock Peters, and *Writing, Plain & Fancy*, narrated by John Houseman, gave Learning Garden an upmarket arty profile. Both films won Cine Golden Eagles. Learning Garden had no debt. I wasn't making a fortune, but it became a springboard to other opportunities.

Bill Davis's talent was sui generis, like no other. I took Bill's work to CBS and landed a job doing the interstitial, "Bumpers," the five-second clips separating the Saturday morning cartoons from the commercials. With Bill's talent, I believed I could pull off an animated project for TV syndication. That year, Mark Twain's story, *Notorious Jumping Frog of Calaveras County*, had gone into public domain. With two award-winning shorts as our track record and the imaginative drawings by Bill Davis, I received commitments from Dan Bessie for live-action and animation direction, and Mallory and Bill for animation. I secured financing for an animation/live-action version of Twain's story. I had followed the same budgeting formula I used for the educational films. That turned out to be a major miscalculation. This kind of animation was significantly more labor intensive, doubling the work hours. At the same time, laboratory costs went up 15 percent. Animation camera services were not giving me any breaks. The enormity of the challenge sunk in. The problem was money. I didn't have enough. As the months passed, Learning Garden was carrying more debt than we could pay at the end of the month.

In 1979, I learned Dr. Tomás Rivera had been named chancellor of the University of California, Riverside. He now lived only sixty miles away. I resisted calling him. I thought it better for him to settle in before I tried to approach him again about his book.

In 1980, Jesús Treviño, a producer at KCET, offered me a job as line producer on his NEH-funded film, *Seguin*. The script was an of-its-time "politically correct" script. But hey, it was a Texas story with a twist on the Alamo. Besides, I hadn't taken a paycheck in weeks from Learning Garden. Other than pace and wring my hands, there wasn't much I could do about the animation for *Jumping Frog*. I tried my hand at animating. I was good at it, but too slow. My time would be better spent earning money to hire people who could do animation faster. I took Jesús Treviño's offer and left Dan Bessie in charge of *Jumping Frog*.

I brought along my Moviola to Texas so we could watch the rushes. The location was Happy Shahan's Alamo Village in Brackettville, Texas, 126 miles west of San Antonio. We filmed on the same set used by John Wayne to make his version of *The Alamo*. Most of the cast and crew were housed in Fort Clark Springs, a historic nineteenth-century army base now a hotel and tourist destination. The days were intense. In August 1980, the temperature soared to 110 degrees nearly every day. The scorching hot earth gave me blisters on the soles of my feet. Everyone had to contend with scorpions in the motel rooms, blister bugs in the woods, and mosquito swarms in the creek beds. We canceled a night shoot because a gully-washing storm turned the once rock-hard desert into three inches of goo.

The cast and crew were dedicated to the project; they gave their best to Jesús Treviño and his script. We had many good days. My friend Lupe Ontiveros was in the cast. I met Judy Irola, Bob Morones, Rose Portillo, A. Martinez, Alma Martinez, Edward James Olmos, Danny de la Paz, Kiki Castillo, Daniel Valdez, and Susumu Tokunow on that show. Bob, Rose, Kiki, Daniel, and Susumu would join me twelve years later to work on . . . *and the earth did not swallow him*.

Jose Luis Ruiz, the local filmmaker who was critical of my adaptation of *Uprooted*, had wanted the line producer job on *Seguin*. As a favor to the director, he was hired as a second unit cameraman. He could have shot sunrises, sunsets, landscapes, wildlife, even a documentary about the making of *Sequin*. Instead, he could be found socializing at the Fort Clark Springs Bar.

My wife Judy visited the *Seguin* set and actually worked pro bono with the wardrobe department for two days. Our children, Rafi and

Rachel, remained in San Antonio with my parents. The show wrapped. Everyone got home safely. My part of the *Seguin* job was over.

While in San Antonio, Judy, Rafi, and Rachel met my grandparents and spent time with my parents. It was an opportune time to talk about a story I wanted to write.

When my father returned from the war, I was five years old. In my father's absence, his younger brother, Guillermo "Willie," had become my play-companion and surrogate father. During the war my father had taken part in the battle for the Vosges Forest in the bitter winter of 1944, and the house-to-house assault on the Alsace town of Ribeauville. Many of his buddies didn't survive. To protect himself, my father had inured himself to death. Once home, he had nightmares that he was back in Germany, snipers everywhere, his death and capture imminent. In those dreams, he feared this time he wasn't going to make it. My father's emotional readjustment was compounded by my uncle Willie's deteriorating health. Scarlet fever had damaged his lungs as a child; therefore, he was 4-F, unfit for military service. A bad flu turned into pernicious pneumonia. It was as if death had followed my father home from the war. Our son Rafi happened to be five years old, the same age I was when Willie died.

The seed idea for *Soldierboy* began to grow. With the wrap of *Seguin*, Judy and I dropped off Rafi and Rachel with my parents in San Antonio. Rachel was two and a half, and my mother was in heaven. We checked in to the Driskill Hotel in Austin, Texas. Three gloriously creative days later we emerged with the first draft of our screenplay for *Soldierboy*.

Back in LA, my absence from Learning Garden had not been good for the *Jumping Frog* project. Dan Bessie was supposed to be in charge but was in a new relationship. Jeez, how dare he try to have a life. I had only been away four weeks.

Due to the *Seguin* and Learning Garden publicity efforts, I was introduced to the team of John Humphries and Gabby Kraft at Universal Studios. I sent them *Soldierboy*. They took a meeting with me, which led to a meeting with Ned Tanen, the head of the studio. He passed on *Soldierboy*, but essentially said, "What else have you got?"

That led me to doing a survey of what Latino projects were out there for the studio to consider. The list included *Bless Me, Ultima* by Rudolfo Anaya, *. . . and the earth did not devour him* by Tomás Rivera, and *Macho* by Victor Villasenor. At the time, Luis Valdez's play *Zoot Suit* was the most successful production ever staged by the Mark Taper Forum.

Zoot Suit, a cleverly constructed musical, was based on the Sleepy Lagoon murder trial in 1943, where seventeen Mexican American young men were put on trial for murder. The evidence was circumstantial and the judge presided over a shameful show trial. Luis Valdez tied the trial to events in Long Beach and Hollywood. White servicemen, mostly sailors from the nearby naval base, armed with pipes and axe handles, patrolled the streets attacking Mexican American young men wearing the popular style for hip young men, the zoot suit. Of course, the incidents were named the Zoot Suit Riots, blaming the Mexican American youth for the beatings they received.

The play opened at the Mark Taper Forum, was extended, and then was moved to the Aquarius Theater on Hollywood Boulevard, where it ran for nearly a year. Various producers tried to acquire the film rights but failed. Interest in a film adaptation evaporated when *Zoot Suit*'s New York Broadway production was met with critical yawns. I took a chance and asked Phil Esparza, Luis's right-hand man, to put me in contact with Luis. I called Luis Valdez and asked him why previous offers to purchase the film rights failed. It appears producers wanted the play, but not Luis Valdez. Ray Stark, a prominent producer at the time, wanted *Zoot Suit* as a starring vehicle for John Travolta. Luis said, "No."

What I proposed to Luis Valdez was a low-budget feature film with him as director. That was acceptable to him. What I proposed to Ned Tanen was the same with a two-million-dollar budget. That was acceptable. John Humphries and Gabby Kraft set up the first meeting with the "principals." That's when things went haywire. Producers began popping up like rain lilies. I didn't have an agent; suddenly I wasn't in line for producer. Ned Tanen offered to pay me for the work I had done, or take a job doing what I was already doing.

I took the money. I needed it to finish the *Notorious Jumping Frog of Calaveras County*. It's not like I neglected *Jumping Frog*. I was there as tired, grumpy animators and painters struggled to the bitter end, and I paid their salaries.

One bright spot: producing the music was a treat. Ernest Lieberman, the composer, had a chance to discuss the score with the conductor before the recording session. This was a union session, with eight musicians, four had never worked together before and were strangers. The musicians were handed the score. The conductor ran though the pieces quickly, pointing out that at this point, the violins should sound like a Scottish bagpipe-like drone, and at this other point, they should play the score as if it were a comic "Turkey in the Straw." After a quick run-through, all the movements were recorded in one take. Ernest Lieberman sang the vocals. I signed the checks, was handed a copy of the score and a half-inch master tape of the finished music. The entire session took less than three hours.

The Notorious Jumping Frog of Calaveras County was one of HBO's first acquisitions for a new form of television called "cable." It won six film festival awards and a Cine Golden Eagle. I managed to pay off all Learning Garden's debts. The economy had taken a downturn. Commercial clients dried up. Finishing *The Notorious Jumping Frog of Calaveras County* had also taken a toll on my relationships with Dan and Bill.

I was ready for a break. Learning Garden was getting banged up on all sides. Filmation, the big animation company, claimed the soundtracks on the "bumpers" we produced for our CBS client were "fuzzed," whatever that meant. The accusation stalled me for days as I chased down the problem. It turned out Filmation was the culprit. The jerks had substituted a "fuzzed" tape for my tape. They assumed I wouldn't notice their bogus tape was not in a Sony box like my tapes. I won big, but why did I have to go through all that?

A project I was developing with Disney Educational suddenly went south. I had put in hours of work on a script, confident that Disney would finance the production. I was blindsided when they suddenly reneged and offered $200 for my effort; meaning they would own my script and the film would never be made. Their offer was so trifling I never bothered to respond. In a pique, I sent the script to Barr Films, a competing education film distributor.

Dan Bessie decided to move to Santa Cruz with his new girlfriend, and Bill Davis received job offers from competitors that I couldn't match. Mallory Pearce, the scientific and medical designer, was devoted to two-dimension animation. Our major medical film client was sold and that ended those assignments. Mallory still had clients, but I had to face reality. I had recently attended a conference where I saw the beginnings of what would become PIXAR. Animators like Mallory Pearce scoffed at the crudeness of the first computer generated images (CGI). I felt differently. The early equipment was pricy, and at that point was not as good, or less expensive, than traditional two-dimensional (2-D) anima- tion. 2-D would continue as an art form, but its commercial future was narrowing. I loved animation, either 2-D or CGI, but frankly, I wasn't a graphic artist. I was a writer.

In 1982, I was forty-one. I'd been in Hollywood ten years and had pulled off some big projects, but I didn't feel that creatively I had done myself any favors. As a producer, I was a glorified production manager. From where I sat, everyone was having fun, and I was paying for it. I needed to concentrate on what I wanted to do, and that was to write and direct.

The time had come to wrap Learning Garden. I ran the company for five years, that was two years longer than the average film production company survives. However, I didn't walk away from Learning Garden empty-handed, I owned the copyright to the films we made.

12

SOLDIERBOY

The reason Zoot Suit, the play, had done so well in Los Angeles was because the production was treated as a cultural event: book and direction by Luis Valdez, music by the legendary big-band leader Lalo Guerrero and the multitalented Daniel Valdez.

Zoot Suit, the film, premiered in 1981. In my opinion, not all agree, the decision of MCA Universal's promotion department to promote the film as a gang movie was a mistake. The ads featured the pachuco, played by Edward James Olmos wielding a switchblade knife. The main character, Henry Reyna, played by Daniel Valdez, was the young man charged with a murder he didn't commit. There were several movie trailers that featured the music and dancing, but the dominant image in all the ads and promotional materials was of the iconic pachuco in a zoot suit.

The problem I had with the studio's sales strategy was that the pachuco's image didn't have the same charismatic allure in conservative parts of the United States. To a substantial number of middle-class Mexican Americans, a pachuco wasn't the essence of cool. He represented drugs, gangs, and prison, not something parents aspired to for their children. The irony was that that those same middle-class Mexican Americans, when they had a chance, identified with the civil rights issues Luis Valdez addressed so successfully, and they enjoyed the oldies music and dancing. The film did well in its initial release but could have done better with the proper promotion. Time has proven *Zoot Suit* a perennial favorite with audiences.

Judy and I submitted the *Soldierboy* screenplay to Luis's producer, Phil Esparza. Why? Because that's what I did in those days. I had nothing to lose and I put it out of my mind. To our surprise, in the spring of 1982, Phil called informing us that Luis had read the script and wanted us to adapt it as a stage play. Luis wanted me, or both of us, to come to San Juan Bautista, California, and work on the play. As I said previously, I was ready for a break from LA. I spent the next seven months in San Juan Bautista as playwright-in-residence at El Teatro Campesino. Judy had a full-time job as an elementary school teacher. She stayed in LA with our children and continued teaching school.

Founded in 1965, Luis Valdez's El Teatro Campesino (ETC) began as an organizing arm for the United Farm Workers Union. As the ETC performers aged and married, the company settled in San Juan Bautista, turning a "packing shed," into their theater. I'm reluctant to use the word "shed," because the building was large enough for a ninety-nine-seat theater, rehearsal space, main office, gift shop, dressing rooms, and ample wardrobe and prop storage. My playwright-in-residence office had been a refrigerator room at one time. My job, while I also worked on the adaptation of *Soldierboy*, was to produce a slideshow for the San Juan Bautista State Historic Park. That turned out to be an enjoyable side gig.

The old Spanish mission, San Juan Bautista, was founded in 1797 and has been in continuous service ever since. The mission was built on a bluff overlooking one of the most fertile pieces of land in the world. The vistas are not grand or imposing, but hospitable and charming. The climate itself was so amenable that people settled there thousands of years ago. Fruit trees grew abundantly. The indigenous people living in the area were friendly and industrious. When the Spaniards saw this paradise, they wanted it for themselves. When the Americans came, they conspired to make it theirs, too.

The hamlet surrounding the mission became a boomtown during the 1849 gold rush. Seven stage coach lines came through daily. The town leaders believed their prosperous town would be the county seat. However, the town's commercial growth came to an abrupt halt when several devastating earthquakes revealed that the bluff the San Juan Bautista Mission was built on was actually *the* San Andreas fault.

Businesses moved to Hollister, eight miles away. As the years passed, the mission, the Plaza Hotel, the stables, storefronts, houses, and much of the old town remained unchanged. Its preservation was partly due to the area's unique microclimate. Summer daytime temperatures were in the seventies. A light sweater was often needed during the day but was necessary after the sun went down. Even with the fault line, people continued to live there. The climate was too agreeable and the land too fertile to abandon. On any given summer day, when the temperature was 72 degrees in San Juan Bautista, in Hollister, the temperature could be in the nineties, or warmer.

During my tenure as playwright-in-residence, on weekends I saw that San Juan Bautista attracted visitors to its restaurants, antique shops, and frontier atmosphere. The old mission had the added appeal of having been an important locale in Alfred Hitchcock's *Vertigo*. El Teatro Campesino produced several plays each year and an annual Christmas pageant that was performed inside the San Juan Bautista Mission. The productions were a big draw on weekends and were a welcome part of the local economy. On weekdays, the town reverted to being a sleepy village off the main highway. Chickens pecked at dead crickets in the street under the lampposts.

I adapted the screenplay on weekdays and drove 315 miles to Los Angeles on most weekends to share the work with Judy. We would work on revisions; then I would drive back to San Juan Bautista on Monday. Luis and I had several consultations. Our discussions were about the mechanics of a scene. I discovered years ago that I thought in visual sequences, like a live-action flip book. As a writer I attempted to translate the visual sequences in my head into words that could elicit those same imaginings for the reader. Writing was the equivalent of sculpting with words. Luis got me to consider what was behind the words, not subtext exactly, but the emotional forces that drive characters to do what they do.

Judy and I submitted our finished draft to Luis for his approval in August. In the meantime, I finished researching and writing the San Juan Bautista State Park slideshow script. This was much like the work I did for educational films; however, instead of shooting 16 mm film, I set up a copy stand and shot all the artwork on 35 mm slides. The finished presentation would be shown in a small theater in the old Plaza Hotel.

Using masking tape, I created the same floor plan for the park's theater inside my refrigerator room. The technology consisted of two slide projectors and a primitive computer where I could sync picture and sound. The slides would dissolve one to the next, and there would be a stereo soundtrack. It was a movie, almost.

Using C-stands and furniture blankets, the El Teatro Campesino sound technician and I turned the refrigerator room into a recording studio, where musician Francisco Gonzales recorded the slideshow score. Years later Francisco would perform the brilliant harp solos for . . . *and the earth did not swallow him*. Luis Valdez also recorded the narration in the refrigerator room.

The "multimedia" presentation, as the local weekly newspaper, the *San Juan Star*, called it, was scheduled to open in September. The slideshow was essentially finished except for glamour shots of the town. I shot several rolls of film at twilight and dawn of the old mission, the ancient cemetery, the nineteenth-century Plaza Hotel and stables that bordered the town's plaza. I felt good about the light and the color of the sky. I dropped the film off to be processed at a professional lab in Monterey.

I woke up early the following morning eager to see the results of what I had shot. There are days in life one always remembers, like my humble, perfect wedding day to my wife, Judy, the days our children were born, and then there was that day in San Juan Bautista. I drove to the lab in Monterey and examined the slides on a light box with a loupe. The colors, exposures, sharpness, compositions were right on. The San Juan Bautista State Park couldn't have been presented better. The slideshow was finished. I was thrilled and hungry; I hadn't eaten breakfast. On the drive to Monterey, I passed a little café in Gilroy, California, called Texas Burgers. I had time and made the stop. Without checking out the menu I ordered a hamburger and sat down. I glanced back at the young woman at the counter. The café's large sign behind her read Tacos de Barbacoa, $1.75. I went back to the order window and asked, "Is that *barbacoa de cabeza*?"

"Yes," the young woman said.

"Cancel the burger and give me three tacos." I was taking a risk, but I had to know if they were the tacos I knew. When the tacos arrived, I was pleased to see the *barbacoa* was served on freshly made corn tortillas. This kind of taco meat is definitely an acquired taste, but I grew up eating *barbacoa* tacos on Sunday mornings; and the Texas Burger *barbacoa* tacos were flavorful perfection. As I paid the check, I told the young woman, "I haven't had tacos this good since I was in San Antonio."

"My father is from San Antonio," she replied.

"Yes, but, I haven't had *tacos de babacoa* this good since I ate at Los Apaches Café ten years ago. The place is gone now," I jokingly added as if I were some kind of expert.

"My father owned Los Apaches," she said. My brain froze for a moment. I took a step back to see the inside of the diner. San Antonio, Texas, in Gilroy, California? It couldn't be, but it was.

When I returned to El Teatro Campesino, Licha, the office manager, accountant, and everything, informed me I had a message to call a producer in Los Angeles. It was Bob Barr from Barr Educational Films. Bob wanted to finance the film Disney had rejected. That was an unexpected surprise. I told Bob Barr I couldn't take the contract, I wasn't available.

"I'll send you a check for $8,000; start when you're ready," he said.

I also had a note to meet with Luis Valdez that afternoon. It was always hard to tell what Luis was thinking. He asked me to sit down, opened a humidor, and retrieved a cigar. He talked as he carefully cut the nib off the cigar. He liked the latest rewrite and he was going ahead with a full production of *Soldierboy* that fall. He lit his cigar.

Okay. Okay. Okay. A full main-stage ETC fall staging?! San Antonio/ *Soldierboy* was coming to California. I may not have been with Judy, Rafi, and Rachel, but that day ranked as one of the best days in my life.

The day of the first read through of *Soldierboy* by the whole cast was another story. For several actors, this was the first time they'd seen the entire script. They might as well have been reading the ingredients on a cereal box. At times the actors took a chance at the interpretation of a line and failed. Those misreadings were like a stab in my heart. At other times their voices found the meaning of the scene and like a zap of high voltage, I was in tears. When the read through ended, Luis Valdez made no comments. The stage manager said we would begin rehearsals the following morning. I was at once euphoric, horrified, and exhausted. It was two in the afternoon. I went back to my room, crawled into bed, pulled the covers over my head, and didn't get up until the following morning.

The *Soldierboy* cast was part professional and part amateur, with two boys who alternated playing Junior, the five-year-old son. Luis treated them all the same. The text was important to him, but more important were the emotions behind the words.

For the first rehearsal of the soldier's homecoming, Luis asked the entire cast to leave the stage. One actor was not among them. Once the cast cleared the stage, the actor playing Frank, the soldier, entered wearing an army sergeant's jacket. Luis had him lie on a table as if he were a corpse; no matter what, he mustn't move. The stage was bare, except for the table and several folding chairs. Tape on the floor outlined where the furniture would be placed. There was a freestanding door downstage.

The stage manager lowered the lights and left one work lamp lighting the corpse. Luis had the cast come in with their eyes closed. Before he let them open their eyes, he told them this is what they silently feared they would see. The actors opened their eyes. Their reactions ranged from gasps to tears. Luis had them close their eyes and the soldier quickly disappeared.

The rehearsal began. In the scene, the characters had been waiting for hours. They're tired, bored, and a little cranky. The stage manager reading the stage directions offstage made the sound of a car stopping with his mouth. Because the actors were watching the stage manager's antics, they didn't notice the actor playing the soldier, Frank, had appeared in the doorway. When Frank knocked, the expression of surprise and relief on other actors' faces sold it. The play sprang to life. Every day during the rehearsals, Luis would create a similar experience for the actors. The play ran for twenty-nine sold-out performances. My writing and directing became markedly better after my experience with Luis Valdez.

I was grateful that my parents, Estela and Severo Perez Sr., were able to travel from Texas to San Juan Bautista to see the production. *Soldierboy* was essentially my father's story. He accepted how we had exaggerated certain things and ignored others. He approved of it. Mom commented that she was surprised that I had been listening all those years ago.

In 1983, *Soldierboy* had a production at the University of Southern California (USC), where our eight-year-old son, Rafi, performed the role of Junior. Productions were also mounted in Sacramento, San Bernardino, San Antonio, and Chicago. The play was published by Arte Público Press in the anthology edited by Dr. Jorge Huerta, *Necessary Theater* (1989).

13

NOTHING TO LOSE

My association with Seguin got me invited to INPUT, an international public television conference. Jesús Treviño had turned down the invitation, so it was offered to me. I was proud to represent the people who made the film, but *Seguin* wasn't my script. I found several "politically correct" passages embarrassing. I did my best to represent Jesús's film. However, I learned the administrators of INPUT were snobbish European academic types who didn't hide their disdain for Jesús's novice effort. I assumed that was the reason Jesús had not come to represent the film himself.

The experience did give me an introduction to the larger world of PBS and the powers that be. When I returned to Los Angeles, I set up a meeting with American Playhouse Productions, of the PBS dramatic TV series. I believed *Soldierboy* was the right project for them. I received a cool brush-off.

Luis Valdez and I tried Universal again, but all our contacts had moved on. *Soldierboy* had an impressive collection of good reviews that didn't mean anything unless they resonated elsewhere, particularly New York City, but we hadn't gotten there.

In the ten years since the book was released . . . *and the earth did not devour him* had become a classic in high school and college classes. If *Soldierboy* wasn't important enough for American Playhouse, what about this book used in classrooms from Oregon, to California, to Texas, to Florida?

I saw something in Tomás's book that no one else I spoke with noticed. The book wasn't a collection of short stories, but a nonlinear novella. The structure was revealed in the first paragraphs of the book, and by the name of the first chapter. An unnamed boy hides under a house recalling fragments of memories of *The Lost Year*.

By 1982, I assumed Dr. Rivera had had time to settle into his position as chancellor of UC Riverside. I had nothing to lose. I called his office and asked to speak to him. He took my call. I explained I was still interested in optioning his book. To my surprise, he invited me to come to Riverside and have lunch. Since 1974, when I had last spoken to Tomás, I'd learned how to option a book. I was knowledgeable about limited partnership agreements, music licensing, distribution contracts, and all the numerous details of producing a film.

For our lunch meeting, I prepared a one-page deal memo outlining that I would pay him $1,000 for a two-year option on his book, with a provision for renewal of the option, and a promise to make a $3,000 payment for the film rights on the beginning of photography. I also brought a check for $1,000.

Tomás took me to the faculty lounge where we had an unhurried lunch. We talked about the recent American Playhouse production of Américo Paredes's book, *With His Pistol in His Hand* (*The Ballad of Gregorio Cortez*). I had heard that Paredes was heartbroken with the production. I thought the film portrayed the Texas Rangers and Texas politics well, but fell down badly at the portrayal of Mexican Americans and Gregorio Cortez. I could see why Paredes was disappointed. Tomás was more generous and said he enjoyed the film.

We talked about writers. I told Tomás about my experience with Victor Villaseñor and his book *Macho*. I had spent an afternoon with Victor, bought him lunch, hoping to option his book. Victor glowed with the self-assurance of a rock star. After all, his book was published by a big-time publisher, Simon and Schuster. He wanted a major studio to option his book. I was small potatoes.

When I raised the subject of an option for his book, Tomás waved away my deal memo and said, "We don't need any legal stuff. You have my permission; just do it."

I explained I couldn't get financial backing for a book adaptation without written permission to do so. "Just do it." He was adamant. No was no. Then came the reason he invited me to lunch, he tried to recruit me to UCR to pursue a doctorate. We parted on good terms. "Just do it," he said again.

I didn't give up. In 1983, I invited Tomás and his wife to dinner at the Mission Inn in Riverside, a hotel popular with celebrities and politicians before World War II. The design was mostly Mission Revival with Moroccan, Italian, and whatever. Tomás called the style *Grotesque*. I made reservations and arranged in advance for the restaurant to charge my credit card. I didn't want the check coming to the table.

Tomás, his wife Concha, Judy, and I sat outside on the patio and enjoyed the evening and the food. Concha embraced us. Tomás and I traded stories about actors and writers. I tried again to get an option on his novel. He said, no. At the end of the evening he had not budged, "Do it," he said. "We don't need signed papers. Do it."

On the second try, he encouraged me again to come earn a doctorate at UC Riverside. I told him I wasn't cut out to be an academic. "Research and writing are fun. I tried teaching. It's hard work if you do it right. I'm a filmmaker," I said. "And I need an option so I can make your book into a film."

"Do it," he said. And that's where we left it. I wasn't giving up.

I had plenty to keep me occupied. After returning from San Juan Bautista, I was busier than ever. I was hired to produce, write, and direct films by Barr Films, Churchill Films, Franciscan Communications, California Department of Education, and several commercial clients. I was working more than before.

14

A DAY IN THE LIFE

I had a full day ahead of me. Not unusual, though I had the extra complication of a construction project. In 1984, my wife, Judy, and I were making an addition to our home to accommodate our two growing children. Our daughter, Rachel, age six, needed her own room, and our son, Rafi, age eight, needed space for his drawing. We were doing the work on a very low budget, with me acting as contractor, hiring the craftsmen and supervising the work. I treated the undertaking like a film production with defined steps leading to completion. Every dollar had to be accounted for.

That morning, as usual, Judy left for work before Rafi and Rachel were off to school. Luis Sanchez, our all-around handyman, and his associate, Manny, were on hold. We were waiting for an inspector to sign off on two jobs: approve the wire mesh for the exterior stucco, and approve the indoor dry wall. We were near to "closing the house," which meant the house was sealed from the elements and ready for occupancy, a step we were all desperately looking forward to. The construction had disrupted our lives for weeks.

Simultaneously, I was doing reshoots for an educational film on CPR for infants. I had arranged for a neighbor with a three-month-old infant to be the model, and brought back Femmy DeLyser, the on-camera talent, to reshoot her scenes. Femmy was a well-known Lamaze instructor and author in the baby-birthing community. Crew call was 9:00 a.m.

The film was a big deal for me. For the first time in many years, the *Journal of the American Medical Association* (*JAMA*) was about to update the guidelines for CPR for infants. I had gotten the very author/doctor writing the new guidelines to review my script. He was credited as a consultant on the film. My distributor was anxious because nationwide advertising was printed, and a release date was set for the following week at a major education market. So, when our consultant, the doctor who wrote the *JAMA* guidelines, sent us last-minute changes to techniques, the distributor freaked. A small part of my film was obsolete. Making changes to an already finished film isn't difficult. However, changes take time. That morning's shoot was scheduled for two hours. The film had to be at the lab by 2:00 p.m. if I wanted a rush order that night. That day's pickup shots were the first of several milestones I had to make over the next several days if I wanted to meet the frantic distributor's deadline.

That afternoon, I was also scheduled to teach a children's class in video-making at Plaza de la Raza, a community arts center in Lincoln Heights. The class was finally getting into the storytelling, and I could blow it with the kids if I didn't show up on time for my four thirty class. I had had some difficulty with this group of children. Their ages ranged from eight to about twelve. One boy, the "cool kid," thought all the ideas for videos were "dumb." The other children were reluctant to speak out and appear uncool.

The inspector said he would be at our house at eight. Luis and Manny had a few small jobs to complete. Essentially, they were just standing by. The hour passed and no inspector showed.

The location for the infant CPR film reshoots was next door on an attractive well-maintained condominium patio by a pool. It was also where baby and mom lived. At nine, crew, Femmy DeLyser, baby, and mom were ready. As I had requested, Femmy brought the blouse she had worn in the previous scenes, so the new footage would match. Femmy handed me a wadded lump. The blouse had been balled up while wet and allowed to dry. Oh, crap. Well, I could deal with it. Fortunately, I had an ironing board and iron next door. I grumbled to myself that Femmy had said she loved the blouse and asked if she could keep it.

I went back home to find Luis and Manny finished with their work, but still no inspector. I dampened the shirt slightly and threw it in the dryer. In five minutes, it would be dry enough to iron. I went to deal with the guys. Luis had other work he could do that day but needed to buy materials. He and Manny took off. Of course, with the lack of space caused by the construction, the ironing board was an aggravation to set up. I ironed the shirt. The wrinkles turned out to be stubborn. I did the best I could on the cuffs and sleeves, since that was all we would see.

I got back to the film crew, and the baby had fallen asleep. Mom was getting a little testy with all the waiting. Bagels, lox, and fifty dollars for her and the baby's time had become an issue. I desperately needed that baby. By now, the sun was overhead. The cameraman informed me that a twelve-foot-square silk screen was needed to soften the light. Putting up a silk screen securely required a bit of Erector Set type of engineering, and because of the small crew it took time.

Eleven o'clock, Luis and Manny were back and working. The inspector was still a no-show. The mom squeezed me for another fifty dollars. The baby was finally awake. Naturally, simple pickup shots became complex. The shots had to be timed to match narration. The baby got hungry and cranky. After several stops and starts, I got the shots I needed. That's when the mom demanded the crew stop work and applaud the baby's performance. She wanted everyone to keep applauding as she retreated to her condo waving the baby's arm goodbye. Normally, I would have been the first to cheer our star's exit. Today, it ate up precious minutes. It was one thirty. I only had half an hour to get the film to the lab. The cameraman handed me raw footage.

At my house there was no sign of the inspector. Luis Sanchez left a message he was going to lunch and would return in an hour. He had finished whatever work he could.

I made good progress though heavy traffic. I was going to make it to the lab. However, the returning traffic on the freeway was gridlocked. I dropped off the film and headed back on surface streets. I pulled into my driveway at two forty-five. Luis wasn't there.

However, the inspector had shown up while no one was around and left a "compliance failure" notice stapled on the wall. Damn!!!! He wrote that we had used the wrong kind of drywall in the stairwell but could proceed with the stucco work. I left a note for Luis Sanchez telling him to wait for me. I would bring the drywall.

I drove to Reliable Sash & Door on Sunset Boulevard. At three fifteen a gaggle of contractors waited to pick up or pay for their materials. I took my place in line. A quartet of sales clerks rotated handling the contractors.

I stewed about what to do. Should I wait? Should I go? If I ran off to teach my class, I would pay Luis and Manny to stand around. If I was late to Plaza de la Raza, the kids could wander off, and I was responsible for them. At this point, I was choosing money over the kids. A headache began to form behind my eyes.

A short, bald elderly man wearing a Reliable Sash & Door shirt with "Richard" embroidered on the chest pointed at me. "What can I get for you?" he asked in an Eastern European accent. I groaned to myself. I got the old, slow sales clerk.

"I need six sheets of fire code drywall." I gave him the specifications. "And I'm late. Can you please, hurry?" He nodded, and walked slowly to the warehouse and ordered one of the Latino laborers to bring the drywall.

"Where's your truck?" Richard asked.

I pointed to my small yellow Volkswagen Rabbit.

He shrugged. He saw my impatience and motioned with his hands for me to calm down. He turned and spoke to the laborers in Spanish. One man produced a large piece of cardboard to protect my car's roof. They circled the car debating how best to secure the drywall with sisal cord. Richard laughed when a man used the word *frenaso*. The word for "brake" in Spanish is *frenar*. The meaning is heightened by adding the *aso*. *Frenaso* meant to brake, as in a hard sudden stop, which would send the drywall flying forward. "*Un frenaso*," Richard chuckled as if the word fascinated him.

As the men went about tying off the drywall, Richard motioned for me to follow him to the cash register. I must have looked at my watch five times in the span of thirty seconds. It was three forty-five. He gestured again for me to relax, that's when I saw a row of faded numbers tattooed on his forearm.

I knew what the numbers meant. I'd seen photos, though I'd never seen them on a real person before. I handed Richard my credit card. As he rang up my sale, I guessed his age to be about seventy. He had been a grown man when the numbers were tattooed. I was thinking about the numbers when he pushed my credit card and receipt into my hand.

"Go," he said.

Whatever anxieties had weighed on me, even the headache, evaporated. Luis and Manny were waiting for me and unloaded the drywall without my having to get out of the car. I made my video class with a couple of minutes to spare.

Somehow, after I had tried for weeks to motivate the students, they let loose and began to allow childhood to return. They joined in improvising and playing the different roles in the video drama they had written. After each shot, they crowded around the monitor to watch the playback. We had a great class.

I never had reason to return to Reliable Sash & Door. It's been over thirty-five years. Our children, Rafi and Rachel, are grown and have their own families. Reliable Sash & Door is long gone. Yet, a couple of times a year when I drive past the vacant buildings on Sunset Boulevard, or when I see someone gesture to calm down a certain way, I think of Richard and a row of numbers tattooed on his forearm. I'm reminded how lucky I was to have a home, a wife and children to share it with, a film to make, and a class to teach.

15

THE RIGHT OF WAY

That same year, 1984, Judy and I made a film about a family of piñata makers in San Antonio, Texas. I wondered if instead of killing a fatted calf, a piñata was a surrogate sacrifice for a celebration to take place. Our children, Rafi and Rachel, and a niece with a few of her friends, were the "party," and the framing device for the film. The subjects were the piñata makers, Juan and Adela Barrientos, a couple almost retired, whose livelihood had come from making piñatas for parties. Their style of making piñatas with *carrizo* (a hardy reed similar to bamboo) armatures may have been unique to the South Texas border. The film followed the couple as they went about the work of making piñatas, from the harvesting of the *carrizo* at a nearby creek, to following the different stages of construction, decoration, and transporting the finished piñatas to market. Of course, in the end the piñata is sacrificed for the celebration.

My brother Rene was cameraman. We shot with an Arriflex camera I borrowed from Churchill Films. The film was shot without sound. I recorded the Barrientoses' interviews in Spanish with a Sony cassette recorder. I transcribed and translated the interviews to English. My friends, Lupe Ontiveros and Abel Franco, professional actors, did an excellent job on the English voice-overs. Marcos Loya composed a sensitive score. I never expected the film to sell big. I did hope that, like *Monitos*, the film might be seen as a document of a specific time and place.

Through it all, . . . *and the earth did not devour him* was never far from my mind. Tragically, in May 1984, at age forty-eight, Tomás Rivera died of a heart attack. I was devastated. We had lost a brilliant, honorable human being with so much ahead of him. I attended his memorial and paid my respects to Concha. Leading Chicano scholars Dr. Luis Leal, Dr. Rolando Hinojosa-Smith, Dr. Carlos Cortez, and many others attended. The event was solemn with choral music and readings. I think Tomás would have enjoyed mariachis, but that was not to be.

One year and a day later, I called Concha and asked her to lunch. After an appropriate amount of time, I asked her for the rights to Tomás's book. She said, she recalled how I pursued the rights before. Tomás liked me, she said. However, another producer claimed he had a signed option. She doubted Tomás would have signed such a document since she had witnessed how adamant he had been with me. She needed to think about it.

Concha called several days later. She had spoken with the other producer. He claimed he had a year left on his signed option. She told him she would give him that year. If he didn't produce a signed agreement in that time, she would not renew his option.

I knew the Latino producer, an American Film Institute grad. We even had dinner after the Tomás Rivera memorial. We both had an interest in the book and he hadn't mentioned anything about an option. He saw the book as a collection of short stories. His intention was to take two or three stories and expand from there. Naturally, I disagreed but didn't tell him. I didn't want him to question for even an instant that he was dead wrong.

Needless to say, I strongly disapproved of Concha's solution. Why hadn't she demanded to see the option right away? If the guy got financing, I'd lose the project forever. In her wisdom, Concha had played it so there wouldn't be any messy lawsuits. One year to the day later, the alleged option never surfaced. I drove to Riverside and had lunch with Concha again. I brought a check for $1,000 and a two-year option in the form of a deal memo. Concha, or the Tomás Rivera Foundation, would receive a check of $10,000 on the start of principal photography. Net royalties from the finished production were to be split fifty fifty.

Severo at age three in a uniform made
by his mother, Estela Perez, when she
worked at a factory making uniforms
in 1944

The photo was used for the poster of Soldierboy, the play, in 1981.

Severo school photo, Little Flower, 1954–1955

Severo, 1967, with Sam the cat

Richard Rodriguez and Carlos Rene Perez, 1967

Teatro Magico, Frank Hein, Bob Isenberg, and Severo, 1968

Burt Lancaster and an extra, 1973

Harry Caplan, Irving Lerner, Caron Beaver, David Miller, Dan Bessie, 1973

Cherry picker, Palmdale, California, 1973

Monitos/figures, 1973, photo credit Judith Perez

Jose Garza, 1973, photo credit Carlos Rene Perez

Uprooted, cast and crew. Standing (*l-r*) Ron Godinez, unknown, Rosamaria Marquez, Severo Perez, Jose Lopez, Alex Balderrama, Linda Dangcil, Rafael Lopez, unknown, unknown. Seated (*l-r*) Estela "Piqui" Scarlata, Julio Medina, Margarita Galvan, Carmen Zapata, Karmin Murcelo.

Severo and Moviola, 1976

Seguin, Brackettville, Texas, 1980, photo credit George Rodriguez

Learning Garden, Mallory Pearce, Severo Perez, Sara Blieck, 1980, photo credit Carlos Rene Perez

Jumping Frog, Wayne Heffley and Adaline Hilgard, 1980, photo credit Dan Bessie

Severo, Judy, Rafael, and Rachel, 1982, photo
credit Maggie Steber

Soldierboy rehearsal, 1981, (*l-r*) Socorro Valdez, Carmen Carillo, Carlo Allen, Beatrice Adame Brown, Al Franklin (in background) Tony Genaro, Luis Valdez, Yolanda Marquez

Judy and Louie, 1982 (Louie was born in San Juan Bautista, California)

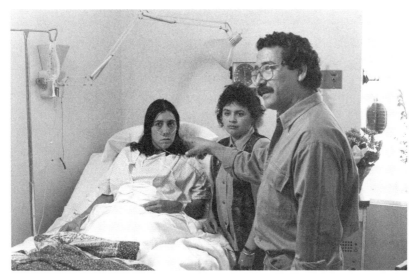

Severo—Hospital scene in *Between Friends*, Tessa Konig-Martinez, Roxanne, Evelyn Cardoza, photo credit Lynn Adler, 1989

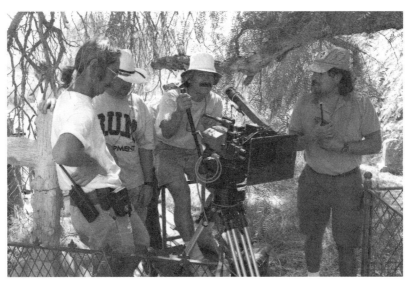

Ron Sill, Virgil Harper, Severo Perez, John Acevedo, photo credit Carlos Rene Perez, 1992

Cast and crew of . . . *and the earth did not swallow him*, 1992,
photo credit Carlos Rene Perez

Severo Perez in 2014, photo
credit Judith Perez

Marcos Loya, 1993

Edward James Olmos (*l*) and Severo Perez, 2019

When you come to the fork in the road, take it!

—Yogi Berra

16

FORK IN THE ROAD

In 1987, I had the option for . . . and the earth did not devour him. What was I going to do with it? My experience at Universal Studios confirmed that public television was my only alternative. Trying to get *Soldierboy* financed prepared me for *. . . and the earth did not devour him.* I learned that good reviews didn't matter; political support got PBS and American Playhouse's attention, but without a public television station producing partner my project had no hope. Other factors could help get a production funded, such as being accepted to a Sundance Institute writing workshop. That would have been invaluable. I had zero pull with those folks. My application for the Sundance scripting workshop was rejected.

KCET, the Los Angeles PBS affiliate, should have been the logical choice as producing partner. Phyllis Geller, their VP of National Programing, was a member of the board of *American Playhouse.* I knew her from several PBS conferences. On a couple of occasions, we found ourselves on the same flight and made plans to share a cab.

A tantalizing prize appeared in 1988: the National Endowment for the Humanities (NEH) sent out a request for proposals to bring literature to the American public in the medium of film. I felt it was almost as if NEH had *. . . and the earth did not devour him* in mind. Tomás Rivera was an inspirational figure, besides being a highly regarded educator, leader, and essayist. Just like that, *. . . and the earth did not devour him* became a viable candidate for the NEH grant.

At the International Public Television (INPUT) Conference in Philadelphia in 1988, I approached the KCET representative about

. . . and the earth did not devour him. She didn't know the book or the author. Politely noncommittal, she asked me to send her a copy of the book and mentioned that KCET was looking at a play called *Roosters* that had a Sundance Institute pedigree.

At the same conference I ran into Paul Espinosa, a producer at KPBS in San Diego. I'd met Paul before and seen his two nationally aired documentaries. They contained good cultural information, with staged reenactments, but the directing and photography were flat and boring. Paul hadn't directed the documentaries. I felt I could do better, and I had a project.

Paul earned a PhD in anthropology from Stanford. Most anthropology dissertations required research into and analysis of the culture of a village. Paul's "village" had been a major television production company. No PBS affiliate station in the USA had anyone like him on staff. I asked Paul to join me for drinks and I pitched the idea of a coproduction by my company and KPBS for the NEH scripting grant. The deadline was a couple of months away, and I had a proposal prepared.

Paul was game. Within two weeks of returning from Philadelphia we had a draft of the NEH application. While I usually wrote alone, my wife, Judy, was my creative editor and confidante. When the draft of my proposal arrived on Paul's desk, it was ready for Paul to do what he did well. He organized the proposal to suit the NEH guidelines. We made a list of possible academic advisors required for the grant. Advisors are supposed to represent a range of disciplines to help guide a project. Paul and I were in agreement in inviting the top scholars in the nation to participate. We ended with a larger than normal advisory panel of impeccably qualified specialists. I feared the many scholarly voices could hinder the project. To my surprise, the advisory panel approved our proposal with positive suggestions that strengthened it.

The NEH proposal went back and forth several times for polishing, until it was unsinkable. We submitted it to NEH in the fall of 1988.

I was approached by the California Department of Education for a gender equity campaign focused on public service announcements (PSAs). The department flew me to Sacramento and presented their materials and content. They wanted me to submit ideas for public service spots. I thought about it and after I returned to Los Angeles, I called them and told them I loved the message they were trying to send to young women and men, but I wasn't interested in making PSAs. They were shocked, then asked what I would suggest. I said the issue was that if Latino parents were reluctant to allow their daughters to go away to college, I didn't think PSAs aimed at empowering young women were enough. The message had to touch the parents, fathers especially.

The half-hour dramatic film that resulted was *Dreams of Flying*. It went on to win five awards for best short fiction, became a successful part of the California Department of Education sex equity campaign, and was repeatedly broadcast on PBS stations for the next three years.

Sal Castro (Belmont High School counselor and the legendary teacher/leader of the East Los Angeles Blowouts in 1968) would invite parents of students to meet to talk about careers and college. He'd give them snacks and show my film about a father who was reluctant to allow his daughter to accept a college scholarship in another city. The story is based on a real young woman whose father, my uncle, refused to allow his daughter to accept a full scholarship to Rice University in Houston. This film was a setup aimed at men like my uncle. The professional actors did an excellent job. The film delivers. Right after screening, Sal Castro would turn to a family and ask, "What about your daughter?"

In May 1989, the NEH project officer, Toby Quitslund, called to inform me that . . . *and the earth did not devour him* won a scripting grant. The exhilaration put me in high gear. I was ready. I had written and rewritten the script in my mind so many times that two weeks after the contracts with SPFilms/KPBS/NEH were signed and the first check had been deposited in the bank, I finished the first draft of the screenplay. I made revisions and submitted the first half of the script to Paul on the following week. I didn't want Paul to think I was knocking the script out too quickly. The script was good. I felt it. Paul liked it, too.

I waited two weeks before sending the second half of the screenplay. Paul knew we had a viable project. We were ready to submit it to the advisors. I altered the title slightly, to differentiate it from the novel: . . . *and the earth did not swallow him.*

Several academics who'd read the novel questioned how the book could become a film. I may brag that I wrote the first draft in two weeks, but I had been collecting notes and writing outlines for years. For me, the novel was an experiential flow of memories, dreams, and flashbacks. The themes in the book were all interconnected. I chose to make the narrator a man speaking of memories he had of his boyhood. Tomás Rivera was between ten and fifteen years old when some of the events he wrote about took place.

For structure, I took the cue from the first chapter of the novel, *The Lost Year*. The events of the past year, tragedies, betrayals, and deaths had taken a toll on the boy, the main character. The novel begins with the boy, whom I named Marcos, hiding under a house, symbolically buried. He struggles to recall an elusive something, anything that might make sense of what he had experienced. He'd lost an entire year, and now the memory returned, not in one piece, but in fragments.

Like the book, the script was written in fourteen chapters. The first and last chapters were the opening and the coda. The remaining twelve chapters (months of the year) formed the body of the script.

Here's one of the truths I learned from Irving Lerner, the director/ editor I worked with on *Executive Action* in 1973: If you want to break with traditional narrative structure, establish your ground rules early. If you show the audience how you're going to tell the story in the first five minutes, you're free to move within those new ground rules. Instead of using chronological events to advance the narrative, the triggers for this film were dreams, flashbacks, and memories.

In a novel, the connections can be made in a sentence. In a film it's done with a visual image accomplishing the same thing by reminding the viewer of salient points. An example of this is when more than three actors are in a scene and only two are talking. the silent actor must be included in the camera coverage. Editors I worked with called it, "keeping the character alive."

The challenge to the one-year, nonlinear structure of *... and the earth did not swallow him* was keeping the story points alive as the film unfolds. I envisioned story elements as threads in a tapestry, with different colors representing the characters, institutions, and incidents of the story. Threads to be "kept alive" had to appear often enough so the audience remembered them.

In *... and the earth did not swallow him*, the Gonzales family lives in Crystal City, Texas. Julian, the eldest son, is in Korea. The opening sequence begins with a montage of images: the audience glimpses Julian dressed in an army uniform bidding goodbye to his mother. He appears next in uniform in a photo on an altar. Julian becomes a drawing made by Marcos at the kitchen table. The drawing then is displayed in Marcos's classroom. Julian's presence/absence is felt in the letters that don't arrive. Julian becomes a letter from the war department. He exists in pleas to the Virgen de Guadalupe for his life. He then becomes silence as the family goes on with their lives. He reappears when the family gives their only photo of Julian to a salesman to be memorialized in a three-dimensional *fotoescultura* (photo sculpture). Marcos finds Julian's photo discarded in a creek. The photo disintegrates when he attempts to save it. Julian returns, but not in a way anyone might expect. Each time Julian appears or is referenced, the content of the scene coincides with another narrative thread: the family, Marcos, school, their migrant life, religion, "superstition," cemeteries, Ramon and Juanita, the moon, and water.

Death too is a thread that exists as an unseen character. I needed to be selective about which deaths I would use in the screenplay. The tragic story of children who died in the fire, *Los Quemaditos*, was too upsetting for me. I couldn't bring myself to imagine or write it. As it is, five people die, all tragically.

No thread is more important than another in this tapestry. The film begins with unresolved fragments. As the film progresses, the fragments begin to reveal more. In the end, the fragments reveal a resolution, though the future remains ambiguous.

Paul had done a superb job of coordinating the complex schedules of the busy academics. They were housed in a hotel where we also held our meetings. The advisors were supportive beyond my expectations. They understood the sacrifices I had to make, such as leaving out the story of *Los Quemaditos*. The book was so weighted down with tragedy, there had to be room for lightheartedness and humor.

Advisor Dr. Nicolas Kanellos defended the ambiguity of the ending. That was a relief. The grand old man of Chicano literature, blue-eyed Dr. Rolando Hinojosa-Smith, thought there was too much untranslated Spanish. I ignored that completely. Dr. Madrid warned that a certain phrase used several times verged on stereotypical. He was right. Dr. Antonia Castañeda thought I could improve on the image of women. I said I would try my best. Other than that, they had only good things to say about the script. As far as the one-year nonlinear structure, the eminent Dr. William H. Goetzmann, professor of American studies, called the script "elegant." If I had been apprehensive that the large panel might be a problem, it was the opposite. They were on board and wrote excellent letters of support.

Since I had finished the script far ahead of schedule, Paul and I had time to rethink our timeline. The step after the scripting grant was the planning grant, which would lead to a production grant. That route would take two years if we were lucky. At any stage, there were no guarantees we would be funded. Since the script was given high marks by the academic advisors, I proposed to Paul that we skip the planning grant and aim for the production grant.

The public television process for creating and funding programming is heartbreaking. Independent producers like me had to make numerous applications, without pay. Having served on PBS, CPB, NEH, and other selection panels, I diligently read dozens of proposals, on one occasion as many as eighty. Of those eighty proposals, thirty would probably have made good programming; ten were outstanding. But only one or two would get funding. And then, it was never enough money to complete the project. Producers had to scramble for grants from foundations and state Arts and Humanities Councils. At a panel I served on, Ron Hull, president of the Corporation for Public Broadcasting (CPB), said, and I paraphrase, "With each round of grants we create dozens of producers who hate us, and a couple of ingrates."

News traveled fast. I ran into KCET's vice president of national programming at another conference. She feigned interest in my project and would "love" to read the script. Perhaps there could be a coproduction with KCET. I learned from another source that KCET was only checking out the competition. They were going after funding from the same agencies we were pursuing, and their project was *Roosters*.

Paul and I focused on NEH, CPB, and American Playhouse. We also submitted to the Texas and California Councils for the Humanities. We crafted the best proposal we could. That was in November 1989. Along the way, I had to write another $1,000 check to renew my option with Concha Rivera.

In the spring, while attending the INPUT 1990 conference in Montreal, Jim Shepard, the NEH literature department director, took me aside and informed me we had been funded for production. WOW.

HOLY SHIT . . . That was an exciting jolt. The announcement wasn't supposed to be public for another month, but Shepard was telling everyone. Paul wasn't at INPUT, so I was singled out for attention. The news was out; I had landed the largest grant given by NEH that year. Two other producers at the conference who had applied for the same grant were informed they had not been funded. I saw the disappointment on their faces. I did not celebrate in Montreal.

A story should have a beginning, a middle, and an end . . .
but not necessarily in that order.
—Jean-Luc Godard

17

RETRACING STEPS

The NEH announcement wasn't public for another month, though everyone knew. The contracts took another couple of months. Naturally, the NEH grant wasn't enough. We had applied for $1,000,000, and were awarded $800,000. That's a lot of dough, but contractually we had to have all the budget in place before we could start production. We did receive smaller grants from the California and Texas Councils for the Humanities, bringing the total to $840,000.

Unfortunately, . . . *and the earth did not swallow him* was turned down for grants by *American Playhouse* and CPB. KCET's *Roosters* won those grants. As a PBS flagship station, KCET Los Angeles had an enormous advantage over me and KPBS San Diego. KCET had a vice president of national programming and a staff. At KPBS, there was Paul, no staff, and me working from LA without pay.

Not that there ever was a possibility that I would work with KCET, but I was lucky to partner with KPBS because they only took 15 percent of the budget as fiscal agent. KCET, I learned, charged a whopping 35 percent.

The monies from the state humanities councils were not encumbered, so I could use them for a location scouting trip. Before I could do any realistic scheduling, production planning, and budgeting, I needed to find actual locations, assess local production services, and check out housing. I had initially planned to see Texas first. I wanted to see the house and neighborhood where Tomás Rivera grew up, but it was September 1990. If I wanted to see the Midwest while it was still green, I had to see it right away.

While writing the script, I relied on the fact that I had traveled through rural Minnesota on two occasions, and I had a feel for the place. I'd traveled through South Texas many times over the years. I produced a segment for the WNET series *Realidades* in 1974 about La Raza Unida party and Crystal City, Texas. In 1980, I worked as line producer on *Seguin,* an American Playhouse/NEH feature film shot in Brackettville, Texas.

I contacted the state film commissions. Minnesota had an office, staff, and a budget to house and entertain me. I was given leads to hotels, farms, crew, and local talent agencies. The Iowa film commission was one guy. I never met him, and only spoke to him on the phone. He was truly helpful, faxing me the names of city managers of the towns I would visit as well as hotels and information about the state.

I arrived in Minneapolis, Minnesota, in late September. My plan was to visit the small towns of Albert Lea and Hollandale, then swing down into north central Iowa.

Southern Minnesota and northern Iowa are similar in terrain, vegetation, and how the land is used. Albert Lea retained a 1950s character. Driving down I-35 toward Mason City, I could see cornfields stretched out like an ocean of green to the horizons. Darker green islands appeared occasionally. These "islands" had in fact been islands before the surrounding wetlands were drained to create the cornfields. Driving up to one of these islands, I found huge deciduous trees, a gabled house, and barns. From these islands it was possible to see two or three church steeples in the distant towns. I took photos of barns, chicken coops, and miles of cornfields.

I drove to Duncan, Iowa, to see the cemetery where our Marcos hid after he was expelled from school. This was a real place. Rolando Hinojosa-Smith, one of the academic advisors and close friend of Tomás Rivera, had provided the information. Gravestones dated back to the nineteenth century. A row of cedars delineated the west side by the road, and tall pines bordered on all other sides. The pines whispered when a breeze kicked up. A huge field of yellowing corn surrounded the cemetery on three sides. In the distance a thresher ingested a swath of corn. It was October 1; the breeze felt icy cold at times. The lush cemetery lawn had yet to experience frost.

On my nightly call home, Judy told me that the comments from the readers on the NEH panel had arrived. She read several. I cried. They said the screenplay was a work of art. I felt vindicated.

I flew to San Antonio from Minneapolis, visited briefly with my parents, and drove to Crystal City. I met Tomás's brothers, Dr. Tony Rivera, the area's only MD general practitioner, and Henry, who ran the local auto body shop. "You bend them, we mend them," his sign read.

Henry was generous with his time, driving me to locales associated with the novel. First stop was the power station where the young man committed suicide, causing a power outage. We then went to the local dance hall. We visited the cemetery where Tomás and *Los Quemaditos*, the children who died in the fire, were buried. Henry took me to the house where the Rivera children grew up, and I saw what remained of the tree Tomás climbed to sit and think in. Many houses in the neighborhood were still boarded up, waiting for their families to return from the harvests.

Henry took me on a surprise visit to a World War II Japanese internment camp that had been in Crystal City. Little remained of any larger buildings, but one housing area stood vacant and decaying. What remained intact like symbols of cultural resistance were two Japanese communal bathtubs, about four feet deep, four by five feet in size.

Henry gave me the names of towns in Iowa, where his family returned year after year. I'm glad I had a chance to spend time with Henry. He had read the book and told me the characters of Doña Bone and Don Laito really existed (Doña Rosa and Don Cleto in the film). They lived in Hampton, Iowa, and their house was probably still standing. The place where the children died in the fire was on Sioux Island. Tomás renamed the locale "Zoo Island" for the novel. That confirmed to me the other stories in the book were mostly true. Throughout the novel, Tomás made references to tragedies and injustices that were common knowledge to Texas Mexican Americans like myself.

I asked Henry about Bartolo Ortiz, the poet mentioned in the book. He had read about him in the book, but Henry didn't recall ever meeting him, which surprised me. Henry suggested I should go to Carrizo Springs and speak with an ex-justice of the peace. He'd been around forever and knew everyone.

The ex-justice of the peace didn't know everyone but knew someone who did, Ben Murray, sheriff of Dimmitt County. Sheriff Murray, a tall, well-built man in his sixties, was a Stetson-hat-wearing, impeccably uniformed, granite-jawed John Wayne type. He spoke fluent Spanish, with an ear for the local vernacular. He sized me up, keeping his demeanor reserved as I gave him my card and told him why I was in town. When I asked him if he knew of the poet, musician Bartolo Ortiz, Sheriff Murray's facade cracked. He sat back in his swivel chair and a smile softened his face. "That man was full of joy," he said.

Sherriff Murray described Bartolo as not too tall, fair-skinned, and wearing baggy clothes. "He'd come to town on the weekends and go to one of the bars, and in a half hour the place would be packed." He played a violin made from a gasoline can, with a wooden neck and strings. He sang and recited poems. Someone would invariably challenge him to *coplas*, rhyming couplets meant to parody, satire, express love or regret. Bartolo would extemporaneously ridicule the challenger's shirt, hat, or his boots. One refrain Sheriff Murray recalled was *Con las botas miadas* (with piss in his boots).

"Bartolo sold broadsides for a nickel about the Cinco de Mayo, or Mexico's Independence from Spain. The poems were fine, not crude or vulgar," assured the sheriff.

He gave me several more leads. One contact was the brother of the owner of a bar named Los Veteranos in Carrizo Springs. Nacho DeHoyos remembered Bartolo very well.

"If you could bottle what Bartolo had, you would have pure joy," Nacho DeHoyos said, holding up an imaginary vial of perfume. It struck me as surprising that both Nacho and the sheriff had used the word "joy."

"The bar owners would bribe Bartolo with all he could eat and drink to have him perform at their place." Nacho added that Bartolo carried a white canvas bag that pulled together with a cord. In it he carried his *sartenes*, metal cooking pans of different sizes that he had made *compuestos*, tuned as instruments. He put the pans on the bar and played them with sticks. He wore baggy clothes, and described Bartolo's skin complexion as *perlina*, a grayish-white like a pearl.

Eddie Sifuentes, the manager of the Texas Employment Commission in Crystal City, also remembered Bartolo and estimated that in 1947 he was in his middle to late thirties. All the contacts described the same wit and charm. Bartolo was beloved.

I was able to spend some time with Tomás's busy youngest brother, Dr. Tony Rivera. Crystal City was lucky to have a bilingual general practitioner with deep roots in the community. We sat in Henry's auto body shop drinking beer. Henry kept the beer cans cold in the soft drink vending machine. He had a key.

Tomás, I was told, was called Tommy, pronounced Tum-meh. They told me the soil around Sioux Island was so "active" it would give you a rash. Workers wore gloves and rolled their shirt sleeves to the wrist. When examined closely, the soil appeared to be made up of thousands and thousands of layers of decaying leaves.

Henry had supported his brothers by sending money orders when Tony and Tomás were in college. "I'd be eating saltine crackers at the end of the month until the money order arrived," said Tony, the doctor.

Tony also knew the novel very well. Because he was much younger, he had been spared some of the hardships his older siblings endured. He accepted the content of the novel as documentary.

Before I left, I visited the grave of *Los Quemaditos*. I wish I could say I brought them flowers. I didn't. I came to explain why they weren't in the script.

I stopped in San Antonio to have dinner with my parents. While dining at Mi Tierra Restaurant, my last chance for fajitas and flour tortillas, I told my parents about my trip and the search for Bartolo Ortiz. When I mentioned Bartolo played a violin made from an oil can, Dad brightened up. He remembered a man who occasionally passed through the produce market. He would play a few songs on the street then go into one of the bars. The people followed.

I had kept notes throughout the trip, shot dozens of photos of cornfields, chicken coops, barns, migrant's houses, and cemeteries. I felt prepared and energized for the next step.

Badges? We ain't got no badges! We don't need no badges!
I don't have to show you any stinking badges!
—The Bandit from the Treasure of Sierra Madre Movie

Badges, to goddamned hell with badges! We have no badges.
In fact, we don't need badges. I don't have to show you any stinking
badges, you goddamned cabron and chinga tu madre!
—The Bandit from B. Traven's Treasure of Sierra Madre Book

18

CHICKENS AND ROOSTERS

The euphoric glow I brought home from my location-scouting trip evaporated when Paul Espinosa called on October 7, 1990. He prefaced his news with, "Just relax. There's nothing to get upset about." That was enough to put my teeth on edge.

Paul had spoken to Lynn Holst, the associate director from *American Playhouse*. Paul was vague about whether Lynn had read the script, but she was responding to Jose Luis Ruiz's comments, and apparently, he had problems with the script.

My immediate response was, "Why the fuck was she talking to him?" I'd known Jose Luis almost from the time I moved to LA. He was the guy who thought my adaptation of *Uprooted* wasn't "barrio enough." Over the years, I had occasional dealings with him. He acted as if he were politically connected, and he might have been. I certainly wasn't, though I didn't lose any sleep over it. His enmity wasn't my problem; that is, until it came to . . . *and the earth did not swallow him.*

Paul and I didn't apply for funds from the National Latino Communications Center (NLCC)[5] precisely because Jose Luis Ruiz was running the place. I don't know what qualified him to be the director of a CPB Latino Minority Consortium, but there he was, and because people talk, I knew for a fact he really disliked me.

---

5. The National Latino Communications Center (NLCC) was one of five minority consortia created by the Corporation for Public Broadcasting (CPB) to develop public TV programs by and about ethnic minorities.

The NLCC's founding mission was to support the efforts of program producers, not be a gatekeeper. Much of what NLCC did was promote Latino celebrities. Which was fine, of course, but if you weren't one of the favored friends or a star, buying a table at one of the NLCC fundraisers might get you a nod of recognition. Judy and I didn't go in for that kind of socializing. I would have welcomed NLCC's nonfinancial support such as publicity and promotion. If Jose Luis had asked, "How can the NLCC be of help?" I would have bought two tables at his freaking fundraisers. We needed an ombudsman. Instead, Jose Luis was an obstacle.

The 1990 National Endowment for the Humanities (NEH) production grant had been an open competition. KCET and *American Playhouse*, with the support of the NLCC, had applied with their project, *Roosters*. When our script won, the rules changed. Paul and I were positioned near the front of line for production funds from the big funders. On its own, the NLCC was not capable of providing any substantial production funds. Their grants were small, usually for planning or finishing funds, and there were twenty or more producers competing for those funds. The crazy thing is I believed that by not competing for the NLCC's meager funds, we were saving funds for other producers.

Lindsay Law, executive director of *American Playhouse*, the PBS TV series that ran from 1982 to 1994, was a cool, standoffish type. It felt to me that after twelve years of running *American Playhouse*, he appeared more bored than engaged with his job. At our first meeting Lindsay wouldn't say whether he'd read the script. However, the implication was that the Latino community, represented by the NLCC, wanted a rewrite. I interpreted Lindsay's meaning as, "know your place and stay in the barrio." I knew we didn't need a rewrite, and additionally, I did not trust nor did I want to be in business with Jose Luis.

The Latino, Hispanic, Mexican American, Puerto Rican, Cuban, Chicano business complicated my life. Because of their proximity to New York and Washington, DC, Puerto Rican and Cuban producers had an advantage with the networks and PBS, although they represented only 13 percent, and 4.5 percent of US Latinos in 1990.

The Mexican American Southwest was home to 61 percent of US Latinos, and most were US citizens. With limited PBS funds only one "Latino" project was funded every couple of years. That meant the

Mexican American Latinos were woefully underrepresented in National programming. The joke among Chicano producers at the time went, "When will PBS hire a Chicano to produce a national series? When they can find one with a British accent."

Roosters, the play, was written by Milcha Sanchez-Scott, who was born in Bali, to a Chinese Indonesian mother and a European Colombian father. She was educated in England before moving to Southern California as a teenager. She was admired and supported by many. I do not question her credentials or her choice of material. The story about a virgin daughter, her cockfighting father, horny brother, and hooker aunt has its place. Odd coincidence, *Roosters* (1987) begins with a sequence under a house that is similar to the opening of Tomás Rivera's book. . . . *and the earth did not devour him* (1971). Both end with a resurrection.

The play's stylized staging with dance and a final levitation was well done, though the fanciful "magical realism" soliloquies, which many people enjoyed, were too "precious" for me. The LA production starred Pepe Serna and my friend Lupe Ontiveros (two fine Texas-born Chicano actors).

Milcha Sanchez-Scott was by no stretch a Latina; however, casting of Mexican American actors made the production a credible Latino funding competitor for grants from CPB and NEH. The producers at KCET had all the big guns in their corner. Besides the Sundance imprimatur, in New York the play had been produced by Joseph Papp and INTAR. In LA, it opened at Latino Theatre Center. The play had enormous backing from the acting community. I envisioned that a *Roosters* film adaptation could be daring and successful.

Los Angeles KCET and American Playhouse were feature film people. They were fairly certain they would prevail. San Diego KPBS, Paul, and I were, well, unknowns.

That didn't deter me. Quite to the point, our submission met the NEH request-for-proposal guidelines, exactly; and that was to bring American literature to the American public. *Roosters* was a recently created play, not a novel used in classrooms across the nation.

KCET and American Playhouse Productions went ahead with a production of *Roosters*. I heard that Edward James Olmos was now involved and was making it his project, with his own director and cinematographer. The NLCC was in full support of *Roosters*, which was exactly as it should be, but why couldn't there be two projects for the NLCC to champion?

Ironically, . . . *and the earth did not swallow him was* American Playhouse Productions' presumptive next project. Lindsay Law, and the producers of *Roosters*, competitors for funding, were now in position to help "shape my script." I was not jazzed by the prospect.

I rewrote several scenes, not for content, but because I thought they could be written better, and hopefully Lindsay would then understand how the script worked. The rewrites didn't satisfy him. He advised me that, "American Playhouse had tried to produce films with nonlinear structure before, and they hadn't worked." I told him that if he wanted to pay me to write a script like *Stand and Deliver*, I could do that, but . . . *and the earth did not swallow him* should stand as is. I was being judged by other producers' failures.

When Lindsay failed to convince me to do his rewrite, he complained to Paul Espinosa in a memo that the script changes suggested by American Playhouse "weren't happening" and the script "was not of the quality expected from me [Lindsay Law] as executive producer." I let that sink in.

In the memo he explained American Playhouse had twelve films that season, and he couldn't take a chance on another failure. *Hot Summer Winds*, a film Lindsay claimed was similar to . . . *and the earth did not swallow him*, had drawn no viewers. He agreed that the way my script as written was justified by the book's structure, but, "Essentially, more artistic kudos I don't need. What I need to deliver to PBS is a bigger audience" (From memo 6/5/91).

Paul was accommodating. He was willing to make adjustments to the script. I wasn't. Paul pulled a power play and refused to pay me for my producer's work until I agreed to rewrites. I stubbornly refused. I told Paul as I had told American Playhouse, "If you want another *Stand and Deliver,* I can do that, but I won't change . . . *and the earth did not swallow him*." Things got rocky enough that we brought in two of our academic advisors as mediators. After all the facts were stated, both advisors agreed my salary should not have been withheld, and rewrites were up to me. In fact, they were fine with the draft as written.

At stake with a rewrite was the nonlinear, one-year structure. I agreed to make some adjustments. That decision would agonize me for a long time. Because of the interwoven story threads, a small change to any scene led to a chain of complications later. By this point, I was ignoring Paul's memos for suggested script changes. It appeared he had forgotten what attracted him to the screenplay in the first place. The revisions took me most of the summer. I restructured the entire screenplay to add a chronological element. I kept much of the nonlinear structure. The changes were painful, but this was a version I could live with. Lindsay Law was still grumbling that my changes weren't enough.

By August 1991, something changed. Lindsay Law stopped bugging me for rewrites. In any case, I wasn't going to budge any further. I believed I needed to stay true to my commitment to Concha Rivera, Tomás Rivera, the book, NEH, the academic advisors, and even Paul Espinosa. I needed to honor the trust they put in the script. We were finished.

In all the meetings we'd had with Lindsay and his associate Lynn Holst in New York and Los Angeles, they never once mentioned *Roosters*, and we didn't ask. *Roosters* should have premiered and begun its promotional tour with Eddie Olmos leading the way. But, nothing.

By the way, the NLCC stiffed me on half the writing fee, about $1,500. Perhaps, that was Jose Luis Ruiz's way of taking a kickback. I didn't make a big deal of it. It was better for him to owe me than for me to owe him.

19

CIRCLE OF CONTACTS

What I haven't written about so far is the film team I had assembled over the years. My closest creative collaborator and editor on scripts has been Judy, my wife. I worked successfully with several excellent cinematographers including Allen Daviau, Izzy Mankofsky, Judy Irola, John Morrill, and others, but Virgil Harper and I clicked. Virgil had made a couple of low-budget feature films. His latest was *Tremors*. He was a visual artist. Nearly all the films and public service spots we made together won awards. Virgil had the reputation of being a bear to work with. I never had that problem. Virgil was willing to do low-budget work, but to do it well, he demanded location scouting and planning. I understood what he needed and made certain we had everything in place for him to do his job. When he finished lighting a scene, he'd turn to me and say, "There you have it, a bucket of art," or a variation, "a heaping pile of beauty." He had several gaffers he liked to use, but our key grip was Gus Vasquez.

My preferred soundman was Susumu Tokunow. A graphic artist in his own right, he also had a superb ear. Besides recording the dialogue scenes, he would collect little vignettes of sound such as a dog barking in the distance, sirens passing, and the ambient tracks. Susumu would squeeze himself in tight filming situations, blending with the crew. On the set he and Virgil communicated silently by eye contact.

I edited most of my own films but worked closely on commercial projects with Susan Heick and Ruth Lee. Both were talented collaborators and fast, superefficient editors.

I contracted with music composers, Ernest Lieberman, Joseph Byrd, Dick Hamilton, and others, early on. They were good and did the work professionally. When they finished, they delivered the sheet music, along with the finished recorded music on half-inch magnetic tape reels.

Marcos Loya and I met in 1982 at El Teatro Campesino in San Juan Bautista. He was lead musician in *Corridos*, Luis Valdez's musical that featured traditional ballads and folk songs. Marcos was self-taught with a primal understanding of sound and music. As lead guitar, he toured with Linda Ronstadt, Madonna, and Chaka Khan. When encountering an instrument he'd never seen before, he'd examine it, pluck it or blow his breath into it. He then would play it proficiently on his first attempt. Besides Marcos's encyclopedic memory of anything he has ever heard, his genius was in being able to watch a sequence, understand its emotional core, then improvise a score with a theme and variations. His preparations were never more than a few chords scribbled on sheet music notepaper. Whatever effort his creative process required, the result was worth it. There was a timeless quality to his compositions that effortlessly suited the film. Marcos chose the recording studios and musicians; I paid the bills. Marcos's *rasquache*[6] style of working was a bargain compared to a three-hour union session. The downside was it took longer.

My brother, Rene Perez, worked as a still photographer on several of my film projects. His archival work was a major contribution to the Willa Brown documentary, commissioned by the California Department of Education. The project required extensive research on Willa Brown, an African American woman who foresaw a future for Blacks in aviation, a new field with no history of racial exclusion. I had never heard of her before but soon discovered Willa had been an audacious pioneer aviator. With her husband, Cornelius Coffey, a licensed pilot and mechanic, they founded the Coffey School of Aeronautics in Chicago. Along with a cadre of likeminded people, their efforts led to the founding of the National Airmen's Association, with members from across the country.

In 1992, when I began my search, Willa Brown had recently died, and Cornelius Coffey was no longer able to communicate, but there

---

6.   *Rasquache* (Spanish). Poor peoples' solutions for scraping by or making-do with what
      you've got at hand.

were six remarkable people still alive who had witnessed this pre–World War II history. The interviewees gave us a warm welcome. Chauncey Spencer (age 92), Lola Jones Peppers (85), Marie St. Clair (75), Harold Hurd (77), Quentin Smith (74), and Simeon Brown (73) had trained and worked at the Coffey School; plus, they were still sharp.

They gave us permission to copy their photo albums and scrapbooks. I paid a photo-use fee to each one whether we used the images or not and promised to return every photo to its original place in their albums. Rene's meticulous methods impressed everyone. He handled the photos wearing cotton gloves. His setup included a copy stand with lights and a glass plate to hold the images in place. Using fine-grained, black-and-white Kodak film, he took several shots of every snapshot using different filters; some of the snapshots were badly faded, wrinkled, and dog-eared.

Once back in Los Angeles, I could see how the filters Rene used were able to bring out details invisible to the unaided eye. I edited the photos into a visual presentation and delivered the research and a script outline to the Department of Education. Approval was going to take time. The scriptwriting would have to wait until the next funding cycle.

My sixteen-year-old son, Rafi, had worked on several of my commercial projects as part of Virgil Harper's grip crew. Rachel, my fourteen-year-old daughter, had small acting parts in four of my educational films. She would soon become an invaluable addition to the wardrobe crew.

I rarely used a script supervisor. They were handy when there was a budget for one. Otherwise, I made notes on my script as I shot.

The individuals named above were my team. We had worked together on many projects, and I trusted and liked them personally. I may have written the scripts, but without the team my films wouldn't exist.

It had been a year since I'd shot an AIDS-themed film, *Between Friends*, with Virgil Harper and a crew. It had been an important film for a difficult time. Death was written on the faces of the men and boys I interviewed.

After *Between Friends*, I needed an uplifting project. I received an invitation to an art opening at the Laguna Gloria Art Museum in Austin, Texas. Carmen Lomas Garza was having a show of her paintings that were illustrations in her new children's book, *A Piece of My Heart* (1991).

Carmen consented to my filming her at the Laguna Gloria Art Museum, her parents' home, the University of Texas print shop, and the Padre Island beach. I booked Virgil Harper as cinematographer and my brother as still photographer. Susumu wasn't available. I hired an excellent sound mixer, who knew he was hired as a fill-in for Susumu. Serendipitous moments happen spontaneously. On the Padre Island beach, Carmen picked up a piece of driftwood and began drawing a hammerhead shark in the sand. Virgil was there to capture it.

Of course, exactly as expected, not long after we returned to Los Angeles from filming in Texas, after being made to wait for two years, I was notified we finally received the green light from American Playhouse and CPB. With our NEH grant for $800,000, we at last had the million we had budgeted. Editing the Carmen Lomas Garza and Cesar Martinez documentaries would have to wait.

Something had happened and I didn't know exactly what. Yes, American Playhouse had put up the money, but it was granted without qualifications. I knew Lindsay Law wasn't satisfied.

In journalism just one fact that is false prejudices
the entire work. In contrast, in fiction one single fact
that is true gives legitimacy to the entire work.
—Gabriel García Márquez

20

PRODUCTION NOTES
PART TWO

It took until May 8, 1992, before we were finally back to work after the previous week's Rodney King unrest. I'd lost eight days of preproduction, but before I could proceed, I urgently needed to deal with Paul. My agreement with KPBS was that all decisions and actions made in regard to *. . . and the earth did not swallow him* had to have my approval. Without notifying me, Paul had sent out a press release announcing the beginning of production of *Tierra*, which was what he apparently wanted to rename the film. That breach of our agreement was bad enough, but he was calling the venture, "The Paul Espinosa Project." What?!

I reminded Paul that our mediation with the two academic advisors still stood. It was my signature on contracts with a KPBS, NEH, CPB, and American Playhouse, not his. I held the copyright. He was calling himself executive producer. I didn't mind the title. If it helped his career, good. Paul may have thought of himself as the brains of the outfit, but, in fact, his Stanford PhD was the all-important muscle.

I know Paul wanted to appear in charge. He had to answer to his nervous KPBS superiors who had never managed a single project this large before. Paul had many important production responsibilities, as did I. As far as I was concerned, the title of executive producer was honorary. We were coproducers. Mentioning the breach of trust to Paul should have been enough. At this point, I had to believe that he would do his job. We were either in sync, or we were going to crash and burn.

What was wrong with *Tierra* as a film name? Attorneys nixed the name because it belonged to a well-known rock group and its product line.

Something I hadn't thought about, even though there was a line item for insurance, I had to take a physical to make sure I was healthy enough for the work at hand. I passed. The insurance company approved me as a risk, so if anything happened to me, the film would get finished without me. Hell, no, over my dead body. No way this film would get finished without me!

Moving forward, I set dates for Virgil Harper, cinematographer, Susumu Tokunow, sound mixer, and my brother Rene, still photographer. Virgil would start in July for a location scouting trip. Susumu and Rene would begin a week before the start date. We needed a production manager, and soon.

Virgil had had the script and my storyboards for months. The SILVERY NIGHT sequence was written to begin in black and white and revert to color at a key moment. I wanted the dream sequences to feel super-real, but flowing and continuous. Texas needed to look different from Minnesota. Virgil did tests with different Kodak stocks and a variety of filters to see how to achieve the desired results.

What camera were we going to use? I had budgeted 35 mm film stock, and Virgil chose a Panavision camera system with its marvelous lenses.

Showing up unannounced at our production office was eighty-three-year-old Harry Caplan, the production manager from *Executive Action*. He still carried himself as if he had something important to do. He'd read in the trades that I was directing a film; congratulations on all that. He'd followed my career. He brought sad news that David Miller had died. Oh, and by the way, he wanted to introduce me to his grandnephew, Barry (not his real name), a production manager. I thought, what a considerate gesture. Barry seemed like an earnest young man. Bob Morones had worked with him before and had positive things to say. I liked Harry. As much as I griped about the experience working with Allen Daviau, he'd given me the opportunity to work with a world-class cinematographer. I had several people in mind as production manager. Each had their strengths and weaknesses. All would have been better than the man I chose. I hired Barry because, sentimentally, I felt I was repaying a debt to Harry. This movie was already a minefield of political, professional, artistic, and social consequences. That wasn't going to change.

I am proud of the actors I chose. I'm quite certain I disappointed a number of talented performers who were competing for those same roles. My friend, Lupe Ontiveros, could have had any part she desired. I wanted her to play one of the women on the migrant truck. With her talent for improv, she would lead the chorus. I told Lupe there wasn't a part, per se, but I would create a character and give her lines. She would get whatever screen credit she wanted, of course.

Lupe looked at me sideways, "What's wrong with the *puta*? I want to play the whore." And so, she would play Doña Rosa. For Lupe to do this part for me was a big favor. We were paying SAG (Screen Actors Guild) scale, which was about a quarter of her usual rate.

We had budgeted SAG scale from the start. There was no negotiating. Actors not so successful as Lupe were thankful for the work. On the plus side, SAG scale wasn't peanuts, and it came with benefits. Our new dilemma was that the two-year delay had played hell with the budget. Costs were up all around.

The first big compromise I made was signing a PBS contract with SAG. The savings were significant in the short run. In a PBS SAG contract, the actors got paid the same, but some of the working requirements were eased; actors would fly coach, not first class; everyone had to share a room; and per diems were smaller. If I ever wanted a theatrical release, all those savings would have to be paid to the actors in one lump sum. That hurt.

The next compromise was that we only had enough money to travel to one distant location, not two. I could find corners of California that could pass for Crystal City and Texas, but verdant moist Minnesota couldn't be recreated anywhere in dry August-September Southern California.

Paul informed me he had accepted an invitation to serve as a juror on a California Council for the Humanities panel. I urged him not to accept. We had a $20,000 grant riding on that funding cycle. Serving on the panel would be a conflict of interest. Paul assured me it wouldn't be a problem. A couple of weeks later he admitted that I had been correct; our grant application had been withdrawn from competition.

By week four of preproduction, crew members were bringing me complaints about Barry, the production manager. Gus Vasquez, the key grip, said our agreed-upon rate was being challenged by Barry. Virgil Harper mentioned that his gaffer was having a similar problem. They felt Barry was trying to get them to quit.

I had a word with Barry. I made it clear these were my team. Whatever deals I had previously negotiated, stood. He apologized and said he was trying to get me the best rates possible. That was acceptable, sort of, except I should have been informed of any crew and budget changes. I didn't like my agreements countermanded.

The people Barry hired were an odd lot, and not in the creative sense. The first location scout he brought me was a burly ex-jock who wore too much cologne and drove me to the location in an aging black Corvette. The location was good: a schoolhouse from 1920 could be redressed as a 1940s barrio classroom. Perfect, except we couldn't use it because the property belonged to Occidental Petroleum and was a millionaire's private playground. That was hard to believe, since the buildings had gone unused for so long that honeybees had lodged visible honeycomb colonies in every wall. Availability should have been cleared before I wasted an entire morning.

I saw several people for production designer/art director. I considered Armin Ganz the leading candidate. I'd seen his work on *Bull Durham*, *Blaze*, and *Birdy*. I was informed by his agent that Armin had recently gotten out of rehab. I hired him anyway. From my experience, a production designer was one of the princely positions on the crew. They dressed with style and had a grand manner. Armin was the modern hands-on type. He dressed professionally, as needed. He had an MFA in architecture and could speak knowledgably about art history or literature. For street cred, Armin had worked as a roadie for the rock group The Band. When I saw how many hours he put in and how hard he worked, I could see how someone could become dependent on stimulants. I didn't ask him to take a drug test as the lawyers suggested. I didn't suspect anything. If he wasn't clean, he was clean enough. I had a good feeling about Armin and entrusted him with a great deal of responsibility. I was lucky to have someone of his experience on the crew. On this, I wasn't wrong.

The next location scout came by way of Armin Ganz's recommendation. She brought Polaroids of a promising locale in Chino, California, which was only thirty miles from downtown Los Angeles, meaning we were within driving distance for cast and crew, saving money.

Summers in Chino are at least 10 degrees hotter than in the Los Angeles basin. The day we drove on State Highway 71 to Chino, the temperature in LA soared to the nineties. There were six of us in the rental van, including Virgil, Armin, the location scout/driver and me. The air conditioner was going full blast but wasn't cooling. The engine sputtered and the van began to slow. The driver turned off the AC. We rolled down the windows. Our efforts were futile. The engine held together until the next exit, and died at the first intersection.

From a moving car, the golden hills of California were distant and pastoral. Inside the stalled van, in 100-plus degree heat, the parched landscape around appeared to shimmer. We sheltered in the van's shade. About a half mile down the road, we saw a Ford dealership, and nothing else.

Virgil moaned, "Well, the middle of nowhere can't be too far."

I had purchased the most powerful Motorola mobile phone available at the time. It was reputed to be for occasions just like this. Portable, yes, but it was the size of a primo cigar box, weighed about six pounds, and the handset was attached with a curly cord. Virgil and Armin teased me about my phone until they discovered their tiny flip cell phones didn't work "near the middle of nowhere." I called information and got the phone number of the Ford dealership.

"Do you have van rentals? My friends and I are in a busted van, stranded off the last exit, at Ramona Road. I can see your Ford signage."

A woman's voice replied, "Yes, we do rent but there aren't any at the moment. Wait. One just came in. If you don't mind it not being washed. We can gas her up and have her ready. We can come get you but it will take an hour."

"No, I can be there in twenty minutes." She asked for my name and driver's license number.

I left my big-ass phone with the driver so she could contact the van rental company and tell them where to pick up their disabled vehicle. The phone was too heavy to carry.

I put on my hat, took a drink of water, and pretended I was walking through a sauna. It wasn't so bad. I noticed that the pastures were defined by slender wooden stakes tied with different colored ribbons, indicating, I guessed, surveying done for future construction.

Entering the dealership, the air conditioning gave me a jolt. The building was so new it smelled of drying cement. The salesman directed me to the back where a lone clerk answered the phone and did the rentals. A cheerful African American woman in her thirties greeted me.

"Where are your friends?" she asked.

"My associates are waiting for me to rescue them." I handed her my credit card and driver's license. "One of the guys said, The middle of nowhere can't be too far. Which way is it?"

She laughed. "It won't be for long. Six months from now you won't recognize this place. So, what are you doing out here?" she asked, cranking the rental form into the typewriter.

"We're location scouting for a movie."

"Really, what kind of movie?"

Outside, I could see a new Ford van being swept out of what looked like feathers. I wondered, what had they been carrying — chickens?

"It's a PBS movie," I answered.

"Really, I love PBS. Watch all the time. What's it about?"

"It's an adaptation of a novel by Tomás Rivera, who was the chancellor at UC Riverside. Sadly, he died unexpectedly a few years back. Did you ever hear of him? His family were migrant workers . . ." I was going to say more, but at that moment a huge teardrop splashed on the rental agreement. The woman grabbed a tissue and dabbed her eyes, then the document in the typewriter.

"Are you all right," I asked.

"Yes," she stopped and reached for a clean tissue. "When I was a student at UC Riverside, my husband and I were living in the married student housing. On Thanksgiving we didn't have much. No turkey. We had frozen chicken dinners. Dr. Rivera knocked on our door and gave us a bottle of wine and a loaf of fresh bread." She needed another tissue as her eyes welled again. She dabbed her eyes and smiled. "I'll always remember that."

The woman handed me the rental agreement. "The keys are in the van. I have your name. I look forward to seeing your movie. Lots of luck."

As I approached the van, what I had taken for feathers were one-inch crescents of white plastic sheeting fluttering around the pavement. Inside the van, it appeared the attendant had swept the crescents out. The van was new. The odometer read a little more than 450 miles.

I started the van and sat there for a moment, amazed by the series of chance coincidences. We kept that van until we started principal photography.

The Chino locale was a three-acre defunct plant and tree nursery on the outskirts of the town. Several small buildings set back from the street could be made to look like Crystal City houses. There were three walnut trees that had been part of the nursery landscaping. After the nursery business closed, the property was essentially abandoned. Apricot, pine, and other trees still in their wooden crates had taken root and grown. The trees were far enough apart and provided enough greenery to vaguely have the feel of smalltown Texas.

I supplied Armin with copies of my storyboards, as well as copies of Russell Lee photos of Mexican American migrant workers in the 1940s and '50s, to use as guides for sets, wardrobe, and vehicles. I also gave him copies of my brother Rene's photos of my grandparents' house in San Antonio. Their living room was frozen in time from the 1940s.

By June, the cast was set for California except for the lead, Marcos, the boy. I made a trip to San Juan Bautista, California, and El Teatro Campesino, hoping to cast one of Luis Valdez's sons as the lead. Unfortunately, the son I was counting on came to the audition with long hair nearly to his waist, a wispy Fu Manchu mustache, and a chin beard. He'd grown a lot since I'd seen him last. I was disappointed that he hadn't read the script I had sent well in advance. Even if he shaved and cut his hair, he was too old.

While in San Juan Bautista, I met with Daniel Valdez, a Teatro Campesino founding member, musical director, and performer. He was the only person I ever considered for the part of Bartolo Ortiz. Danny wasn't a *huero* (fair skinned) like Bartolo, but he had magnetism.

When I returned to the Chino location several days later, Armin had made architectural sketches for my approval. The only difference from reality was that he made the set about 5 percent larger than normal size. He had staked out the best angles for backgrounds and sunlight. The UNDER THE HOUSE set would be built from scratch and be tented to control the light. The trench would be dug so the camera crew wouldn't have to crawl around on all fours and would be wide enough for a dolly to move. The EXT. FAMILY HOUSE and the EXT. NEIGHBOR'S HOUSE would essentially be false fronts added to the existing structures. The FAMILY HOUSE would include working windows and doors so actors could enter and exit. However, the interiors would be shot on a soundstage elsewhere.

Before the location could be used, the buildings had to be fumigated for an infestation of black widow spiders. Everyone was warned. Watch where you put your hands and do not go exploring.

Paul was in San Diego most of the time and didn't see firsthand what Armin, Virgil, and I were doing. Paul wanted me to rewrite the scenes to cut back on the expensive sets. I had already done that. I was well aware of the cost of construction. We couldn't cut costs across the board. The decision should be how important was any set to the overall story. The Chino location worked as the opening and closing of the film, as well as SILVERY NIGHT and RAMON Y JUANITA. We were scheduled to be there six out of fifteen shooting days.

It was at about this point I chose to forgo my director's salary. I would take payment at the end. There was a good chance I might not be paid at all. However, my decision immediately added $90,000 to the budget. That's a lot of money, but to earn it, I had to work three years. I knew this was something Paul wouldn't volunteer to match. After that, Paul was on pretty good behavior.

By July 4, Bob Morones was freaking out. The start date was closing in and we hadn't cast our lead, Marcos. I had seen scores of boys. The problem was the character didn't have many lines and was in almost in every scene. He was the witness who carried the burden of the story. Most of the boys we saw were like child models, perfect for catalogs and store ads: cute, but couldn't act.

Paul Espinosa was holding up his end keeping payments and salaries flowing in proper order. We were making progress with locations and were on schedule for an August 11, 1992, start date.

Virgil Harper, Armin, and I made a location scouting trip to Minnesota. I had wanted to film in Garner and Duncan, Iowa, but the distance from a major airport made shooting in Iowa prohibitive. After all, sugar beet fields were sugar beet fields whether in southern Minnesota or northern Iowa. In a couple of days, with the aid of the Minnesota film commission, we secured the locations we needed.

I got it in my mind that a farmer in 1952 would either own a newish postwar tractor or a prewar tractor. I asked the older farmers that question wherever I went and had yet to receive a definitive answer.

On our last outing, the day had gotten late enough that we could have headed back to the hotel. I still had two tractor leads I wanted to follow up. Virgil was fine. He was driving. Armin was getting testy. I asked if he needed a pit stop and he said, no. In his opinion my pursuit of antique tractors was a distraction. My first lead was a tractor dealership, and yes, he had some older models he was restoring. They were completely inoperable.

Armin grumbled that he could find tractors. He'd rather be making phone calls at the hotel. I had one more stop, a pig farm. The landscape was flat and treeless with several warehouse-style barns, and neat metal fencing all around. The enclosures were reasonably clean for a pig farm, except they retained the fine pig aroma.

The owner of the place was Hans Becker (not his real name). Hans was a small man, maybe five foot three, in his late sixties. He wore workman's gray twill shirt and pants, and a cloth World War II Wehrmacht-style cap. He eyed us suspiciously as we approached.

"Mr. Becker?" I asked.

"Yes." He appeared guarded.

"I'm Severo Perez, and these are Armin Ganz and Virgil Harper. We're a film crew location scouting."

"You can't film here. No movies." Hans waved us away. "No movies here. Pig farms not treated fair. . . ."

"No. sir. No movies here," I assured him. "I understand you have antique tractors. I was hoping to see them."

"Tractors," Mr. Becker's eyes popped open so wide I could see the whites around his gray-blue pupils. "You want to see my tractors?"

"Yes, sir. We heard you had older models, antiques."

"You want to see them now?"

"Yes, sir."

Mr. Becker excitedly led us to a long warehouse barn, opened the door, and turned on the lights. By his count he owned over forty-five tractors of all makes and sizes. Mr. Becker took us on a tour. This barn held about fifteen. His oldest, from 1915, still worked. In fact, they all worked, and he had to start them and drive them around every month so they remained in working order.

"I've loved tractors since I was a little boy," he said. "I used to run home from school before it got dark. My father would let me do two or three rows before it got too late."

"I have a question. What kind of tractor would somebody around here have in 1952?"

"Why?"

"Because in the story, which takes place in 1952, when the actors have a scene, we see a tractor in the background or working behind them. How old would that tractor be?"

"Nobody had new tractors until later. It would be like this John Deere 1937, or maybe like this 1939 Farmall. You want to use one of my tractors in a movie?"

"Yes, sir. If you give us your permission. We'll pay, and we have insurance. They won't be doing anything dangerous."

Virgil Harper, who owned a farm in Oregon, was considering buying a used tractor. Hans Becker followed us to our car enthusiastically offering suggestions. They chatted until we had to drag Virgil away.

As we drove back to the hotel, Armin apologized. "I take it back. This stop was worth it."

Getting back to Los Angeles, Bob Morones was in a panic. "Urgent. Let's talk boys. I have a suggestion." Bob had narrowed all the auditions down to two boys that read well, and were the right age. They were at the top of my list as well, without much enthusiasm.

Bob wanted me to talk with them. I auditioned them again. One enunciated clearly, but couldn't give me an expression to go with the lines. The other boy had a thick East Los Angeles accent, but a transparent quality. If I suggested what he was to feel and think, I could see it on his face. I took them out to dinner with their parents. The character didn't have many lines, and his face was essential. I chose Jose Alcala, the boy from East LA. I hired the other boy to be part of the chorus of workers.

There were two rehearsals with the actors, and a read through with the entire crew. Meetings with the prop master were like visiting a candy store.

I didn't have a lot of time to reflect during the next two days. The last details were getting nailed down. I felt Barry, Paul Espinosa, Bob Morones, and Carolyn Hale, an associate producer, were in sync and in control. At that moment the collective enthusiasm was high. The cast liked the script; the key crew members felt like the film was an important project. I felt solid going in. We had the resources to do this and were ready to go.

Two thoughts were on my mind on the eve of August 11, 1992. First thought, besides Virgil and Armin and the other principals I would deal with personally, the rest of the crew had been hired by Barry. I approved them, yes, but I didn't know them. They were gnarly, grizzled types, veterans of many crews. I felt like a sea captain setting sail with a crew of pirates. Second thought, I had become hypersensitive to gratuitous flattery. Some compliments were a courtesy, like when an actor makes positive remarks about the text before they read. That's expected. However, praising a modest suggestion I made as if it were a grand epiphany, made me uneasy. It happened too often from set dressers and prop persons, I felt as if my options were being curtailed, because my suggestion was now the be-all and end-all of options. I suspected they were flattering me so I wouldn't change anything.

Besides these reservations, I was amped. I couldn't wait to start the first of twenty-five shooting days.

I thought about how I would like to edit this. I wanted the film to flow like a symphonic journey. I felt it should have a heartbeat: 68 beats per minute to start, increasing quickly to 72, then 80, then back to 68. I started a chart of the heartbeat changes from scene to scene. Okay, that was enough overthinking. I finally fell asleep.

On the first day of production, you forget about the film you want to make. You won't see it again for a long time, if ever.

—Anonymous

21

THE RESURRECTION

By necessity, the scenes in a film are shot out of sequence from how they appear in the script. To make the elements of a scene (props, costumes, makeup, body positions) match when edited, we relied on the script supervisor's notes, our collective memories, and hundreds and hundreds of Polaroids. The script supervisor, the prop and wardrobe departments strung the Polaroids by scene numbers on metal hoops. Any details germane to continuity were written on the back with a Sharpie. The cataloging with Polaroids seemed like a burdensome waste of time and money until the moment you needed them. Then, they were indispensable.

The first day's shooting location was EXT. CREEKBED. The set was dressed and ready for shooting at call time. In this sequence the boy follows a small snake in a creek, which leads to the discovery of his brother's photograph, which disintegrates when the boy tries to rescue it. Because the scene involved splashing through a slippery creek, following a snake, discovering the photo, shooting could have been tricky. Virgil and the grip crew made it look easy. We got lucky. All takes were good, and I had several good options. Nailing the first shot was an adrenalin moment. The next several scenes went well, too.

With the first location came the first disaster. The grip truck was driven into an area not suitable for heavy vehicles and got stuck. Luckily, we were able to make changes in the schedule and continued to the Chino locations to shoot exteriors. Okay, not to dwell on mishaps, but what the hell happened? Paul appeared reluctant to tell me the truck couldn't move because it had a busted axle. Barry blamed the driver. We lost precious time.

The first scene we shot at the Chino set was the final scene of the film. The boy climbs the tree and waves at an unseen person. I called the sequence THE RESURRECTION. It was stressful to shoot, and not because it was difficult. Everything I would shoot over the next twenty-five days, everything I'd planned for, was leading to this moment in the film. What I saw while shooting was good, sincere, restrained, but I didn't know what I thought. When I called "cut," every face on the set focused on me. The scene looked fine, but could I do it better? I waited a moment and finally said, "We've got it. Check the gate. Moving on."

Day two, was the UNDER THE HOUSE sequence. The reality of the 80-pound Panavision camera was frustrating me. The rig didn't float like a butterfly. A 160-pound dolly and dolly track were necessary everywhere. Camera setups could take half an hour, often longer. Virgil had planned for these camera moves, and I had approved them. Still, I felt I'd given up spontaneity. I wanted to move a lot faster.

By Friday we were already behind schedule because of the broken axle nonsense. We had planned a night shoot for Friday to coincide with the full moon. The scenes we lost to the broken axle had to be shot during the day. The Friday night shoot was moved to Saturday.

Saturday's scenes, the SILVERY NIGHT and the NIGHT THE LIGHTS WENT OUT, were part reality, part dream sequence, and I wanted to give them all the time needed to get them right. Considering that we were planning to use a crane/dolly combination with the 80-pound camera, we would need about four hours for shooting after 8:30 p.m., when it would finally be sufficiently dark. That meant I needed the boy until 2:00 a.m. All parties were okay with my plan, except for Screen Actors Guild. At the last minute SAG informed us the boy could not work after 9:00 p.m. We appealed, arguing that the boy was fourteen. The shoot was on Saturday night. We were doing nothing dangerous, and we weren't working on Sunday. Monday was a light day for the boy. The SAG response came as two words, "*Twilight Zone,*" the film that tragically killed the actor Vic Morrow and two children in 1983.

I had to finish with the boy by 9:00 p.m. Seven shots, seven setups in a half hour, that was crazy. I timed the narration several times to determine the variables. Seven camera setups became two tracking shots.

Virgil ordered a second dolly, laid out two setups while it was daylight, and we rehearsed. We had planned for a full moon. We got a little bit less, but close enough. The scenes worked. There was one wardrobe change. We got what we needed in two long dolly shots, one with a crane. The footage came out better than I had originally planned. No one from SAG made any noise when we wrapped the boy at 9:45 p.m.

Rafi and Rachel, my teenaged kids, had jobs on the film. I can't say too much more about them because I hardly got to see them during working hours. They became an integral part of the production. Rachel worked in the wardrobe department and took on the big responsibility of dressing the extras. Rafi painted sets with Armin Ganz's art department. I know they worked their hearts out, and I saw the results of their efforts every day. They made me proud; they were exactly where they were supposed to be, working behind the scenes.

The day Lindsay Law showed up at the Chino location, the temperature was 110 degrees. A strong wind came up and, unexpectedly, a twenty-by-twenty-foot silk screen took off like a kite. The crew scrambled about like ants grabbing at C-stands and flags. When I finally shot the scene, the cast did an excellent job. I hoped Lindsay saw that, too.

The troubles we were having were production manager Barry adjacent. He apparently made deals with the pirate crew, and some of the cash-strapped pirates were slow to make good. He threatened to replace them, causing tension. More than that, there were three major logistics foul-ups pointing to Barry. The first was the broken axle on the first day. The second foul-up sent the wardrobe truck to the wrong location. Thank goodness for my big-ass phone, the wardrobe truck finally was able to locate us, but we lost two hours of shooting time. Scenes that didn't get shot that day had to be added to the schedule while we were still in California.

Two days later a third foul-up, the camera truck was sent to the next day's location instead of the location where the crew and I were waiting. I lost another two hours. I threw the only tantrum I've ever thrown as a director. It didn't get me the camera, so the outburst was wasted.

Barry pretended he didn't know what had happened to the camera truck. Knowing where the equipment was all the time was his job. I fired him. How he treated the crew was reason enough to let him go. More Barry problems were uncovered by our production accountant. He had damaged my reputation with businesses by claiming they had competitors who were bidding lower than our prearranged agreements. I don't know if he was angling for kickbacks but his behavior wasn't acceptable. I had to call old acquaintances and remind them it was me, not Barry, they were dealing with. Whatever amount of money he might have saved the production in renegotiated deals, we lost more through his incompetence.

Carolyn Hale, the associate producer, told me privately it was Barry who had handed out the wrong call sheets. Paul should have been on top of that. Producing was a big job. Mistakes get made, but you can't keep secrets if you want people to trust you. I hoped these types of breakdowns wouldn't happen again. We made some staff shifts and moved on. In any case, our logistics problems pretty much resolved after that.

Armin Ganz's sets existed solely for the film. The kitchen and bedrooms were sets on a soundstage. What was seen through the windows were theatrical backdrops with painted landscapes. The actual exteriors were the buildings in Chino, California, with the augmented facades. Because of the Polaroids and Armin's talent, everything matched and flowed seamlessly from exteriors to interiors.

Rose Portillo's powerful performance as the mother is the very heart of the film. Marco Rodriguez became the father, humble, brave, and caring. When on the set and in costume, he remained in character. If you saw him away from the set, he was often difficult to recognize.

Art Bonilla and Evelyn Guerrero were suburb as supporting cast. Linda Dangcil played *Hermanita*, Little Sister. When we were to shoot her scene, I said, "Bring that magic I saw at the audition."

"That's the easy part," she teased. "Is there anything else?"

After Barry's departure, the pirate crew wasn't quite so surly as before. They still complained and weren't the kind to be flexible with the rules. An example of their complaints: "The last film I was on the producer flew in fresh crab from Alaska." Yeah, right. On one late night shoot, after having to change locations due to rain, all the nearby shops and restaurants were closed. Paul, the associate producer and I made bologna sandwiches on white bread with mayonnaise for the crew.

Working on a fixed budget and schedule, shooting numerous takes of a scene in order to get it right is equivalent to making the same mistake over and over and expecting a different result. My job was to deliver the actors' performances and their coverage. I would always try to get a clean take of everything, but if a take started weak but got stronger as it played out, and if the next take started strong then fell apart, I devised a third shot that tied those two takes together and accomplished the sequence. Several times while the camera was rolling, I'd see a moment, a smile or a reaction that I might be able to use, and even if the rest of the shot wasn't perfect, I would circle that take.

I had been lucky finishing the SILVERY NIGHT and NIGHT THE LIGHTS WENT OUT sequences by 9:45 p.m. I had time to rehearse. With the other missed sequences, we had to steal time from other scenes. The same attention to detail applied to wardrobe, lighting, camera angles. The difference was I only had a few moments to rehearse and shoot one, maybe two takes, tops; then move on. A couple of times I had to accept what I got. The WHEN WE ARRIVE sequence escaped me all together. I would have to find another way of creating the missing scene.

Like the character, Candide, in Voltaire's novella as he descends a precipitous mountain, I too was losing some of my precious cargo.

22

THE WRAP AND POST

Going into the last ten days of shooting, in terms of success, I got the best I could. Lupe Ontiveros, Sam Vlajos, and Sal Lopez were excellent as murderers and victim. The boy, Jose Alcala, did a fine job as well.

The compromises I was forced to make in Minnesota had nothing to do with the cast, crew, or producers. When organizing the shoot, we planned for three cover days in case of rain. It rained six days out of ten. At night at the motel, I rewrote exterior scenes for the following day as interiors.

My big losses were the scenes we never shot because of the rain. There was no budget for another day. Once I changed the schedule to assure the key scenes were shot, three scenes became my Sophie's Choice. The DINER, the KRESS STORE, a PHILOSOPHICAL MOMENT of a character taking a dump: these scenes were never to exist. They were important threads in the tapestry. Their weight was in how they set up or informed a character's behavior. The mother's story was going to be left unexplained. A viewer might not miss it. I would and did.

Several people have pointed out that in one scene during a rain-storm as the family huddles under blankets in a leaky shelter, "At least, you used the rain to your advantage there." No. That was fake rain, shot on an overcast day. It looked real because Armin and his crew made it look so. Filming with lights during rainy weather requires many precautions. We did shoot while it was raining, but not scenes with rain. Rain is unpredictable. It can come down in torrents, or just stop when you need it. It's more efficient to know exactly when and where the water is coming from, and where it's going. Actors must be kept a safe distance from electrical currents.

We wrapped production on a high note in Minnesota. The MIDWEST SCHOOL scenes went very well. Armin's sets were exactly what they were supposed to be: a 1952 school, the nurse's office, a classroom, the principal's office, the boy's restroom. It felt as if I had opened a copy of a 1952 *Saturday Evening Post* magazine and stepped into it. Virgil, the cinematographer, was excellent to the end. Performances were strong. For my part, I tried to keep the heartbeat of the story animated.

Paul Espinosa, Bob Morones, Carolyn Hale, and several production managers did a fine job getting us in and out of Minnesota efficiently. We had a small wrap party in Minnesota on the last night. The pirates spent the evening making contacts for their next gigs. The following morning, everyone went their own way.

Back in LA, I rented an editing room in Burbank and hired Susan Heick as editor. She brought in a super fastidious assistant. The guy was a maniac for keeping things neat, which was fantastic because his logs made it easy to access any scene and take, quickly. However, he would have paroxysms of indignation if I touched the film boxes myself. Without exaggerating, he would pace the floor, wring his hands, and complain to Susan that I was touching the film. I tried explaining that I was a filmmaker. I knew how to maintain logs and could operate the Moviola. I was also the film's writer, director, and producer. He thought touching the film was his domain alone. It was a union thing.

The two-year delay waiting for the green light, the rain, the scheduling mishaps, meant we went over budget. We needed $250,000 to complete, that would also finally cover my deferred salary. KPBS and Paul couldn't cover $250,000, so editing would shut down until the next funding cycle.

I left the assistant editor to his job because I needed him to rush a rough assembly. I had given Susan a list of the takes I wanted her to look at. She chose to use master shots and ignored much of my intended coverage. We were under pressure, and she never got around to them, though that was unusual for her. I missed her energy and imaginative spark. The problem was that Susan and her husband had *just* adopted a three-year-old Vietnamese orphan. By *just*, I mean within a couple of days after we started editing. The child spoke no English and had never seen an American-style toilet before. He would pee in the corner of his room. Susan had a lot on her mind, and it wasn't my film.

I had my first meeting with Marcos Loya, the composer. He immediately came up with an idea for the opening. He connected his electrical pickup from his guitar to a cassette recorder and improvised a tender evocative guitar solo, which eventually became the film score. When he thought he had captured the essence of the sketch, he ended with an extended chord, not really part of the score, but a way of saying "like that."

Lindsay Law came out to see the rough cut. I assumed as an executive producer he'd seen rough cuts before. From other producers, I was forewarned that with Lindsay that was not the case.

As a producer, I warned inexperienced clients that a work print was a work-in-progress. I explained that grease pencil marks indicated dissolves and fades in the final film. I told them they might also see scratches and splices. I assured them that none of those defects would appear in the finished film. Invariably, when a grease pencil mark appeared on the screen, the client would leap from their seat. "What was that?" I'd explain that those were the grease pencil marks for picture dissolves I'd warned them about. After all that, they would anxiously ask, "Will that be there in the finished film?"

It turned out Lindsay was like one of my naive clients. A rough assembly is just what it sounds like. All the scenes are assembled in order for the first time, mostly using the master shots. At this stage, it was absurd to attempt fine tuning.

We had five days to pull something together. I synced the guitar sketch that Marcos Loya had improvised the first day. I explained to Lindsay that what he was about to hear was unfinished temp music improvised by Marcos Loya. The guitar flowed with the images effectively ending with Marcos's prolonged chord and out. I left the chord in because it provided an ending.

At the end of one scene, the assistant camerawoman ran into the shot and made a tail slate. Lindsay sat up, "That's not going to be there?" I explained that we left in the woman doing the tail slate because for those two or three seconds, there was recorded sound I was planning to use. Another image, to be added later, would replace the assistant camara woman. It was a rough cut!

Lindsay didn't recall I had mentioned it was temp music. "I was enjoying the music when suddenly, boom a strum and out. It was dreadful." I explained again it was temp music, and this was a rough cut. Paul had been silent thoughout the screening and didn't say what he thought of the rough cut.

"Cut five minutes, and you're through." With that, Lindsay made his exit. I ignored his ridiculous remark about being through. I had a feeling that from the start Lindsay had hated the film and having to finance it. My rough assembly had proven he was right. I knew the film wasn't anywhere close to being finished. As expected, funds were cut off and editing shut down.

I hadn't been paid since May and it was October. The production had used my big-ass cell phone and it accumulated a $1,400 bill, and I had another $2,200 in expenses that needed to be reimbursed. I expected all of that would have to wait for the next funding round. KPBS could not cover my salary, but it did pay my large phone bill and reimbursed expenses. Paul was scrupulous about getting receipts for everything, and because I wanted Paul to be perfectly honest with me, I accounted for every cent I asked for in reimbursement.

To secure finishing money, I had to show CPB and NEH a film that looked ready to go; the editing wasn't there yet, and no one was offering a hand.

There were dark moments. I didn't know what would happen next. Had I completely fucked up? Judy came to my rescue. She asked, "Do you believe in the film?" Yes. "Then take $20,000 from our savings and finish it."

I rented a one-bedroom bungalow in Hollywood. The place had been another producer's office that hadn't been used in a while. Limp macramé plant holders hung by the patio door. This was probably a thriving flower-child production company in the 1960s and '70s. The bungalow's bedroom was the editing room. The tiny living room was an office/den, and then there were the necessities: the kitchen, bathroom, and telephone. The small patio had gone unattended for some time. I brought over a Weedwhacker and swept.

I purchased an eight-inch candle, the kind in a glass jar with a label dedicated to a saint. I turned the saint to the wall and attached a post-card-sized photo of Fellini directing Anita Ekberg, which I had clipped from a magazine. I lit the candle when I arrived in the morning. The flame burned away the bungalow's musty odor. I brought my portable radio tuned to two stations: KUSC (FM), classical music, and KFWB (AM), all-news radio. I played the radio when I was alone. Music was great for certain kinds of work, and all-news radio because it repeated traffic and weather information every twenty minutes. KFWB reminded me there was a world out there that had little or nothing to do with me. It had welcomed me home to Los Angeles during my long drives back and forth from San Juan Bautista. It was the radio station I tuned to as I drove through the LA riots. I found it comforting.

I spoke to Paul on a couple of occasions and told him what my plans were. He was an employee of KPBS. He wasn't able to come and see how the editing was progressing.

Susan Heick wasn't able to return, which was a relief. Susan and I would work again in the future; for now, she was living the life challenge she had asked for. Like the consummate pro that she was, Susan introduced me to her replacement, a wonderful guy, Howard Heard. He immediately took charge of the film, arranging the 35 mm boxes of work print according to the assistant editor's fastidious logs. A 35 mm Moviola was brought in, and we got to work.

Howard was the enthusiastic ballast I needed. He was the first to tell me, "Forget what you didn't get. Celebrate what you have." We tackled every sequence, "keeping the narrative threads alive." There was a series of steps. We started by assembling the film into fourteen chapters/movements. The chapters were then edited to work as stand-alone pieces. The chapters were then refined to work with each other, as how one flowed into the next. We made the scenes take shape. It was all there. Well, almost.

I got to use those shots that had a special glance or reaction, which I had circled while shooting. What Howard noted was that the scenes as reedited were actually longer, and because they played better, their length didn't matter. We created ambient and special effects tracks. The dialogue tracks were split to have better control of all voice levels. We then did rough mixes in preparation for test screenings.

The . . . *and the earth did not swallow him* NEH production budget still had money for a scheduled meeting of the academic advisors. I screened the work print and rough mix for the scholars while we could still make changes. As a whole they made positive remarks. Julian Olivares made the most important comment, "Fix WHEN WE ARRIVE and you've got it." Of course, that was one of the scenes that didn't get shot.

Early on, I had a problem in that the boy had a very strong East Los Angeles accent, and that wasn't the voice I wanted to narrate the film. I had Bob Morones bring in men for the NARRATOR. One of the men who auditioned, Miguel Rodriguez, had a contemplative engaging voice. I hired him to do the temp narration. Miguel came in, did the reading, no muss, no fuss. He was good. He was gone.

Howard and I finished a cut that looked decent. Lindsay Law, in town on *Rooster* business, dropped by to take a look. I had screened the film for Paul prior to Lindsay's arrival. I told him what we had done about pulling the alternate takes, followed by the quick sound mixes, and how this made the film feel tighter.

When Lindsay arrived at the screening room, Paul surprised me by launching into how "WE" had pulled alternate takes, done some quick mixes, and "WE" had made the film tighter. Not mentioning that he had nothing to do with the edit, and that I had paid for the entire effort.

After the screening Lindsay declared, "I'm glad you took my advice and cut five minutes." Only Howard and I knew the film was actually twelve minutes longer. I did a quick transfer to VHS, and though we weren't through editing, that was the version we submitted to CPB for a finishing grant.

On October 31, 1993, the composer Marcos Loya and I sat in the bungalow in Hollywood on a Sunday afternoon. On Friday, Howard and I had finished editing. The picture was locked. I was showing Marcos changes that would affect scoring. When we finished the music cue sheets, I turned on the all-news radio. Marcos took out a joint and leaned over the eight-inch candle for a light. The flame unexpectedly flickered and went out. At that instant, the KFWB announcer said that Federico Fellini had just died. Marcos and I looked at the candle. I decided not to relight it. Marcos's temp music included click/rhythm tracks that would serve as the underpinnings of the soundtrack. The time signature matched the action of the scene. The bass track, in a sense the heartbeat I'd imagined, would be recorded first, the film score would be built from there.

Word came down from American Playhouse that our film didn't have any stars. *Roosters* had Edward James Olmos and Sonia Braga, international movie stars. We had a talented cast but no stars. Their recommendation was that we hire someone like Hector Elizondo, the esteemed actor, as star narrator. I had Bob Morones send Hector the script and a VHS with Miguel Rodriguez narrating.

Hector responded promptly. These are not his exact words, but close, "Your narrator has done an excellent job. I won't replace him." For people who know Hector Elizondo's history, his response was expected. He wasn't going to replace a capable actor just because the producers wanted a star. I was thankful.

We were awarded the CPB finishing grant, which meant I was finally paid my back-salary and the $20,000 I borrowed from savings. Work that still needed to get done were five sequences requiring optical effects: the desaturation of the SILVERY NIGHT scene from black and white to color; one freeze frame; two fades; and a series of complex dissolves for the opening and closing montages. The opening and closing credits had to be designed and shot. These were some of my favorite activities. The businesses that provided these services were in the neighborhood.

We could now pay Marcos's contract, hire musicians, and book a recording studio. For the next two months we were in and out of a sound recording studio in Granada Hills, owned by patient and talented engineer Jay Bolton. Jay lived in a ranch-style house, on land that had twenty years before been an orange grove. He had taken the two-car garage with an attached apartment and rebuilt it as a state-of-the-art, attractively appointed recording studio. His clientele were famous and not-so-famous singers and groups. The citrus trees remained part of a well-maintained landscape surrounded by a lush green lawn. His backyard was bordered with high Ligustrum hedges, which provided privacy. There was a swimming pool and a bathhouse in case an artist desired to take a dip.

Recording and mixing with Marcos was a roller coaster ride. His challenge was enormous. The highs were awe-inspiring; in the lows he would lose his temper with me and Jay Bolton, whose family needs interfered with Marcos's crazy schedule. I never doubted for a moment that Marcos could deliver. I knew he would. I had to keep him together for the film's sake and his sake. I had craft services, coffee and pumpkin empanadas ready at the start of each business day. I spent hours babysitting Jay's two-year-old toddler, so Jay could remain at the recording console.

At the same time, the music Marcos created was inspired. The musicians were at their best. He wrote *Tierra* (the film's main score and its variations), *Mama's Theme, Don Cleto's Polka, Dona Cuquita's Cumbia, Mud Fight Guapango, De Trabajo a Trabajo* song; a total of forty-six original cues, some used more than once.

The performances were concert level: Joe Rotundi, keyboard; Francisco Gonzales, harp; Geree Gonzalez-Contreras, vocals, Robert Peralta, guitar; Val Salazar, *bajo sexto*; Louie Mendez, guitar; and Emilio Armijo, accordion. Marcos played the Spanish guitar, *requinto romantico, jarana, quatro Chicano*, Native American flute, and percussion. We finished recording over the Christmas holidays and had a chance for a breather before the next step.

Perhaps, the earth was getting ready to swallow someone. On January 17, 1994, I was in Oakland, California, having dropped off my son, Rafael, at his dorm at the California College of Art. I was staying in a nearby motel, woke around seven and turned on the TV. It was still dark. The images on the TV screen were of natural gas fires and crumpled buildings. I turned up the sound. A major earthquake had hit Los Angeles. I tried calling home. The circuits were all busy. Damn, I had forgotten to bring my big-ass phone.

At dawn, the TV cameras revealed the devastation was widespread. One of the spans on Interstate 5 had collapsed. The freeway was closed, which definitely affected my drive home. News was still sketchy. I couldn't stay in Oakland; I had to make it home. I knew my diesel-powered Volkswagen Rabbit pretty well. I had a full tank, which meant I needed to stop for one fill-up before getting within fifty miles of LA. I tried calling home several times with no luck.

At the Coalinga rest area, I was able to call home from a pay phone. Judy and Rachel were okay. However, the cats were freaked. With the closure of Interstate 5, my option was to drive east on State Highway 14, around the Angeles National Forest mountain range, and enter Los Angeles County from the southeast. That wasn't a route I'd taken before. It would add about 200 miles to the trip.

There were scores of cars at the rest area. People gossiped and repeated what we heard on the radio. I saw fear in the eyes of teen girls waiting in line to use the pay phone. I had the feeling the place could get creepy if the intense transient gathering lasted more than a day. On State

Highway 14, the traffic slowed to a crawl. I was finally within the broadcast range of Los Angeles's KFWB all-news radio. It informed me I was in a twenty-mile-long stop-and-go traffic jam. At that rate, I would surely run out of gas. I saw a motel and convenience store and pulled over. I bought some chips and a couple of beers and checked into the motel. The TV news images were more graphic than before, and were repeated over and over. By 3:00 a.m. the traffic had cleared. I took off. I was able to buy diesel at the next intersection. I arrived home about 6:00 a.m. The cats had calmed down, and thankfully, Judy and Rachel were safe.

Regrettably, things were not good at Jay Bolton's home and recording studio. Granada Hills and Jay's property were at the epicenter of the Northridge earthquake. For several days, I couldn't get it touch with Jay. Marcos and I had no way of knowing if our master recordings had survived.

When I finally saw Jay, he described the earthquake's sound as a deafening train roaring through his bedroom while the entire house shook violently, punctuated by the trill of glass breaking. Outside his bedroom window he saw the water from his swimming pool rise into the air like a wave and crash against the house. He heard someone screaming and realized it was himself. Jay, his wife, and toddler daughter were traumatized but unharmed.

His studio was a catastrophe. Miraculously, our master tapes weren't damaged. With the music score completed, the soundscape was about to take shape.

23

WHEN WE ARRIVE

The final sound mix was done at Cinesound on Highland Avenue. I'd used this studio exclusively for years. I knew and liked all the mixers. The cool poster designed by Bill Davis for *Astronauts and Jelly Beans* hung in the Cinesound bulletin board the year the film won a CINE Golden Eagle.

I needed an industrial dolly to carry in about 150 pounds of bulky 35 mm film reels, the mixing elements for . . . *and the earth did not swallow him*. In volume, they took the space of a large steamer trunk. The sound mix was a big job. The first thing Cinesound did was to rerecord the original quarter-inch tapes on 35 mm magnetic film.

I arrived the following day and found what I thought were homeless men camping out in the soundstage. They were Foley artists, and the old clothes were a necessary part of the job. For two days these men became quite intimate with my film. The men created the sound for any object that moved, flapped, or fell. It was best not to watch them because, what they did was rather like playing an instrument, except with objects one couldn't imagine could make such sounds. It might look like he smacked a metal trashcan with a hose, but done precisely so. If you were watching the screen it would sound like a car door slam. One run-through was footsteps. The Foley artists walked on different surfaces, recreated echo effects, stepped through crunchy leaves and spongy wet grass, all to film playback. The next pass included mattress spring squeaks. Another pass was for clothing, fabric rubbing against fabric. One man got on his hands and knees on a pallet filled with earth to duplicate the sound of the boy crawling under the house. They also created the sound of bodies moving during sex in a trailer.

The next day the Walla[7] crew arrived. I had scripted parts for them. Their voices prayed during the opening sequence; they called for "Marcos" during a dream sequence. They provided the grunts when the tired migrants stepped off the truck and created background chatter when there was a crowd. I scripted a short piece for a female actor catching a rooster and carrying it off to make dinner. I also scripted the WHEN WE ARRIVE speech and chorus to use over a montage of traveling shots, which took the place of a scene that did not get shot because the camera truck was sent to the wrong destination. Yes, we were still paying for those foul-ups.

Enrique "Kiki" Castillo and his wife Bel Hernandez, both fine actors, were a special part of the Walla crew. Their voices created the boy's conscience. They did wonderfully, exactly what I needed. And, after all these years they still haven't forgiven me for not casting them in the film.

The final mix was the culmination of all the work of many artists and technicians. When we began the mix, there were about thirty-five tracks, We were mixing in twenty-minute sections, the length of a standard 35 mm reel. In the Cinesound engineering room, a bank of reel-to-reel playback machines ran the sound tracks synchronously, making a deafening clatter when they were all engaged. Twenty feet away, the mixing studio was completely soundproof. This was the best of midcentury analog technology. When work finished on a twenty-minute section, the reel-to-reel playback machines were unloaded then reloaded with the next twenty minutes. I became conscious of how future projectionists were going to make reel changes.

The sound designer, Mark Rozett, mixed the thirty-five tracks down to something manageable. One mix was ambient atmospheres, birds, insects, dog barks, and mattress squeaks. I really loved that. The Foley and Walla tracks followed, then the dialogue and music tracks.

The final sound mix was done at night. On exiting Cinesound at 2:00 a.m., I discovered that nighttime Hollywood was nothing like daytime Hollywood. In the daytime, the neighborhood was all business: an

---

7.   "Walla": film term meaning the murmur of a crowd in the background.

unpretentious commercial dry cleaner across the street, a lunch joint at the corner, car rental offices, small studios, and several soundstages in very ordinary looking buildings.

At 2:00 a.m., cars lined up at a valet parking stand on Highland Avenue. At night, unused soundstages were turned into peripatetic, impromptu clubs with disc jockeys. Young women wearing skimpy dresses and heels stepped out of cars as their young men stood by looking bored. There was a festive vibe as a line of revelers waited to enter the club. What I had thought were decorative artifacts on the buildings turned out to be lights that illuminated the street and buildings.

The following morning the valet parking stands had disappeared. The sidewalks were swept clean and the streets clear of the nocturnal denizens.

Two nights later, we mixed the final reel. We were through. I was asked to step out of the mixing studio so the room could be "painted" with "pink noise," whatever that meant. I was told it was to allow me to hear the full effect of the sound system, Ultra Stereo, a less expensive alternative, but technologically equivalent to Dolby Sound.

What followed was the run-through of the entire film and the Ultra Stereo master. For the last several weeks, I had only seen the film in twenty-minute segments. This wasn't one of my educational films. Was it the film I had wanted to make? That didn't matter anymore; this was the film I ended up with; and like my children, it had my DNA.

The film started to roll and it wasn't going to stop. All decisions on picture and sound had been made. The title, the credits, the optical effects were finished and inserted into the work print. There were no grease pencil marks. There wasn't another thing I could do, or say. Long ago, maybe when I decided to give the film a heartbeat, I began to think of the film as a character. And like one of the actors or crew, it had looked to me wanting to know what I wanted it to do. It spoke through the cinematographer, the sound mixer, the prop man, the art director. "What do you want me to do?" This sensation had intensified in the last days of sound mixing. A glass of water placed on the floor asked, "Louder, less loud?"

As the film continued to roll, I was watching my child walk away. It was no longer looking over its shoulder asking, "What should I do?" It was going its own way, living its own life. I wanted to shout, "Please remember to call."

Just as the LA riot and the earthquake were the sign of the times, so was postproduction sound. From the time I wrapped principal photography to the time I finished editing and started the sound mix, a sea change in technology occurred. The digital change had been coming; we all saw it. I needed an industrial dolly to carry the heavy boxes of 35 mm reels into Cinesound.

Over one weekend, Cinesound transferred all my 35 mm magnetic reels to DA 88 digital tapes. A DA 88 tape was smaller than a box of regular-sized Bicycle Playing Cards and could hold eight tracks. I may have walked into Cinesound with an industrial dolly, but I left with a small box holding six DA 88 tapes: the newly mixed master in Ultra Stereo, a version for a foreign language dub, backup copies, and all the mixing elements.

Cinesound embraced digital technology, though digital technology did not embrace back. Cinesound closed in 1996.

One day the analog world that thrived for at least half a century disappeared altogether, and only a few old guys like me remember. Am I sad about this loss? In fact, not at all. Much of the expensive time-consuming optical rigmarole, like "freeze frame wedge tests," were now a matter of a click on a keyboard. Gone was the special shelving required to hold hundreds of feet of carefully cataloged motion picture film, and stored in boxes. Every sequence was an easily accessible file in a folder on your computer desktop.

Nothing is permanent. Whether it's Indonesian shadow puppets, Greek dramas, or my dream for holographic movies, the medium will change. It's the stories that will remain the same.

24

THE WAY HOME

I first processed film at FotoKem Lab in 1973 when it was a startup film lab on Cahuenga Boulevard at Barham Boulevard. On one occasion, the screening room was under construction when Reg Dunn, the general manager, screened my answer print[8] on the back of a door. Of course, Reg denied my recollection ever happened. He was proud of his immaculate screening rooms. I also believe he loved filmmakers. When I landed my first large contract, CFI and Deluxe General, the major labs in town, would not extend credit. They would process my film, but it was COD. Reg gave me credit. Over the years I brought all my commercial business and personal work there. Reg occasionally would drop by the screening room to see what kind of film I was working on. I made artful, well-produced films and paid my bills on time. By 1992, FotoKem had become a major lab and video transfer service. While I was working on . . . *and the earth did not swallow him*, Reg Dunn gave me generous access to their screening rooms and projectionists.

The response to the . . . *and the earth did not swallow him* was good from NEH and CPB, but not so much from KCET and the NLCC. Considering how coolly they treated me when we had to interact, I was grateful they were leaving me alone. On the other hand, they were publicly funded institutions that were supposed to be supporting independent producers' efforts. The majority of the cast and crew lived within

---

8.   An answer print is the first version of a motion picture that is printed to film after color correction of the original.

KCET's broadcast area; that alone should have been reason enough for the station's support.

. . . and the earth did not swallow him premiered at the Santa Barbara Film Festival in April 1994. Before the festival, an article in the *LA Times* by critic Gregg Barrios gave us a publicity boost. The turnout was so large the festival booked an extra screening. Even so, dozens of disappointed people were turned away. If I were to do it all over again, I would schedule a special screening for cast and crew. They are there to see their own contributions. Other than the key department heads, many of the crew never read the entire script. What was tragic or subtle on the screen might have been hilariously difficult to accomplish behind the scenes. The chuckles were subdued and limited to three or four crew people; however, for me their reactions were a poke in the eye. The film won the Audience Award, which came as a complete surprise.

Paul, regrettably, was making decisions independently again where my input had been contractually required. I would have liked to have a say on the one-sheet lobby poster he commissioned. Its design wasn't bad, but that wasn't the point. It was my decision to make.

Paul and I were approached by Tom Garvin, an agent who represented films to film festivals. He sent promotional information to all the major film festivals in the world and offers came in. We accepted his offer, only to discover later that his services weren't cheap, but they were effective.

A few days after I returned from Santa Barbara, I received a phone call from Frank Mancuso Sr., president of Paramount Studios. It wasn't a secretary, it was him. His gruff, gravelly voice barked, "This is Frank Mancuso from Paramount Studios. I would like to take a look at your film." Naturally, I got the film to the studio that same day. The following morning, I received a call from Mancuso. He announced, "Your film is a work of art. Paramount doesn't distribute art. It's not for us. Thank you for sending it over." I wasn't all that upset. I was glad to have gotten a straight response. Those are rare. I knew from the start it wasn't a studio picture.

In 1994, my father, Severo Perez Sr., was diagnosed with advanced pancreatic cancer. What made the period at all tolerable for me was that he was able to see the completed film on a widescreen TV. He was quite weak but was grateful. We had talked about the making of the film many times. After the screening, he called me to his side. "The scene with boys fighting in the bathroom, that was me," he confided. Yes, the scene came from the book, but I staged it from an incident he told me about when he was a boy.

He died in November 1994. Among his things, I found he had kept a scrapbook of all the newspaper articles, film festival schedules, programs, and publicity flyers for *Soldierboy, Unrooted, Seguin, The Notorious Jumping Frog,* and *Astronauts and Jelly Beans.* While Mom had worried that I'd come to a disastrous end, Dad reveled in the fact that I took chances despite the risks.

There was something else that brought me down, though. In the period that followed the premiere, I went through what I think was similar to postpartum depression. I had been like a pregnant mom filled with life-affirming hormones, and suddenly the hormones were gone. I had worked on the project for so long, I had become addicted to the drive to get it done, the adrenalin rush, the pressure. At the time, I couldn't define what was happening to me. Add to that a series of disheartening events.

An agent called wanting to represent me. That should have cheered me, except, he sent me out on a several interviews. What I encountered was what I expected. As one TV producer said with no malice, "When we need a Latino director, I know I'll have another choice." The reason I'd gone my own way my whole career was because of that attitude. I didn't want to be the minority hire. . . . *and the earth did not swallow him* had typecast me as a Latino director. That was the gist of how the interviews went. I told the agent I wasn't interested.

At about the same time I received a letter from Frank Pierson, president of the Director's Guild, inviting me to become a member. To this day I regret that I never replied to the invitation. I was simply too depressed. That was the problem of going it alone. The upside, of course, was I got to produce films I wanted to make without having to answer to anyone. The downside was that when I made a mistake, I owned it completely.

A friend sent me a copy of an Albuquerque, New Mexico, newspaper with an article about Paul Espinosa's new award-winning film, . . . *and the earth did not swallow him.* My friend called a couple of days later to rub it in. "Your name wasn't mentioned in the article. He's taking sole credit. I thought you wrote and directed."

That was really a shame. Paul was smart. By giving himself executive producer credit, I hoped he realized he was setting himself up to become a national PBS producer. But no, for some misguided reason he wanted to be me. His new honorific was *filmmaker*.

In 1993, I received a piece of good news. Funding for scriptwriting phase of the Willa Brown documentary came through from the California Department of Education. For my mental health, I needed the challenge. The interviewees, Chauncey Spencer, Lola Jones Peppers, Marie St. Clair, Harold Hurd, Quentin Smith, and Simeon Brown were now two years older and frail. Others on my list to interview were either no longer lucid or had died while I was trying to locate them. These folks were the story. I urgently needed to get these people on film.

I used my writer's fee money to fly Virgil Harper, the cinematographer, my brother Rene, and a soundman to Chicago, then Lynchburg, Virginia. I brought gifts of the 8 × 10 blowups of photos Rene copied on our previous visit. The cleaned-up photographs of the gatherings and special occasions reawakened Depression-era memories of triumphs, friendships, and rivalries. I gathered more material than I could possibly use in a half-hour documentary. Their story was undeniably important. The Chicago aviators, Willa Brown, the Coffey School of Aeronautics and their advocacy group, the National Airmen's Association, had led to the creation of the legendary Tuskegee Airmen.

I contacted the CPB Black Minority Consortium about this history. I hoped to find a producer who could take over the project. I believed the material could be expanded into a longer feature-length documentary. Conversations went nowhere. The half-hour documentary commissioned by the California Department of Education, *Willa Brown: An American Aviator*, narrated by Debbie Allen, was distributed to PBS stations across the United States. Within a year, Chauncey Spencer, Harold Hurd, Simeon Brown, and Lola Jones Peppers died.

The 1994 screening of . . . *and the earth did not swallow him* at Kennedy Center for the Performing Arts in Washington, DC, was the moment Paul and I got to show NEH, CPB, and Congress what we had done with their money. The screening was coupled with the National Hispanic Media Coalition Conference, a group advocating for the inclusion of more Latinos in the media. Paul and I stayed at the Watergate Hotel, which was weird enough.

Kennedy Center for the Performing Arts was a modern, austere building on the Potomac River. The screening room held about 400 people and was packed. In attendance were dignitaries, several congresspersons, all the big funders from American Playhouse, CPB, and NEH. Judy's aunt and cousin, two Washington, DC, insiders, were able to attend. At the time, Judy's cousin, Lois Schiffer, was serving as US Deputy Attorney General for Environmental Affairs in the Clinton administration.

Paul thanked the appropriate funders, including the NLCC. I fumbled through a thank you to Concha Rivera, the cast, and crew. Naturally, the sound and picture at Kennedy Center were superb.

The next evening, Paul and I were scheduled for a Q&A session and book signing. Arte Público Press had published a special edition of Tomás Rivera's book with my brother Rene's production photos on the cover and inside. As the Q&A wrapped up, someone took over the mic and the event devolved into a birthday party for Jose Luis Ruiz, the director of the NLCC. A long line of people stood waiting to have their books signed as the boisterous birthday salutations made it impossible to speak.

25

ONCE AROUND THE BLOC

Many screenings followed, including at the Director's Guild, Lincoln Center, the Detroit Museum of Art, the Museum of Modern Art, the Houston Museum of Fine Arts, and the Smithsonian. I did screening fundraisers for the United Farmworkers Union throughout California, Washington State, and North Carolina. There were too many college and university screenings to remember them all.

Over the next two years, the film screened in at least twenty festivals. The Moscow International Film Festival was noteworthy. They paid passage for two. I took the opportunity to take a side trip with Judy to Helsinki, Finland, before continuing to St. Petersburg and Moscow. A Finnish filmmaker friend, Markku Onttonen, had invited us to visit for several days. Markku produced quirky, humorous dramas for Finnish television. His mother had been a nationally acclaimed folksinger, and he was an officer in the Finnish National Guard.

Markku and his wife immersed us in Finnish culture. They served me reindeer meat for breakfast. Judy, a vegetarian, ate scrambled eggs and cucumbers. Apparently, there weren't many vegetarians in a land with a short growing season.

They lived in an efficient mid-twentieth-century-style home bordering a forest. We drank vodka, showered, indulged in their sauna until we glowed with perspiration, showered again, and dove into their cold indoor pool. Wrapped in terry-cloth robes, we drank more vodka by the fireplace next to the pool. Naturally, Markku and I talked about movies. What Judy enjoyed was a jog on a trail through the birch forest outside.

The Finnish countryside consisted of forests, numerous lakes, and fields blanketed with yellow-blooming rapeseed. Helsinki was a combination of ancient, historically important, well-maintained structures, and newer architecturally attractive buildings. Every place we visited was immaculately clean.

Finland was a first world country. The United States was not third world, but it wasn't first world by Finnish standards. Besides English, Markku and his wife were fluent in their native language, German, Swedish, and French. Markku's wife was a high school biology teacher, a highly respected profession. The country had national health care, one of the best educational systems in the world, and their Nokia cell phones were far more advanced than what was available in the United States at the time. The supermarket I visited with Markku was comparable to one in an upscale neighborhood in the United States, but with high-tech scales and scanners.

Our last night in Helsinki, Markku wanted to have a vodka bonding. To show my gratitude for his hospitality, I agreed, but only until it got dark. Before I knew it, it was 3:00 a.m., I was slurring my words and it wasn't dark. It doesn't get freaking dark in Finland in July. Judy and I had to be up at 6:00 a.m. to catch the train to St. Petersburg. Somehow, I did it, like a zombie, but I did it. A spotless Finnish train took us swiftly and silently to the Russian border. The Finnish border agent stamped our passports and asked where we were going. I said Moscow. He handed me back the passport and said almost as a warning, "Lots of luck."

We had hired a service to help us when we arrived in St. Petersburg. Once we cleared customs, a woman who spoke limited English took us to our hotel. She would return in two days to take us to the train station. We were on our own. We were booked at the Grand Hotel Europe. The exterior and lobby were old-world "grand." The guide said the nineteenth-century hotel had been renovated. Perhaps so, but our room furnishings were threadbare. There was CNN and pay TV. St. Petersburg is a handsome city. If you squint, and I did, the place could easily be placed in the seventeenth, eighteenth, or nineteenth centuries. By the end of the twentieth century, the neighborhoods lacked maintenance. Western-style consumerism had arrived in post-Soviet Russia. Marlboro, advertised as "the American Cigarette," and Coca-Cola ads adorned billboards and bus signs everywhere. It was interesting to think that nicotine, caffeine, and sugar water were the American entries into the Russian marketplace. Japan, on the other hand, competed just as heavily with Sony and Panasonic ads.

Ordering dinner for me was easy; for Judy it became a challenge. On our first night at the hotel restaurant, Judy ordered a pasta with no meat. The waiter brought pasta with sausage. Judy said she couldn't eat meat. "Not meat," said the waiter, "sausage." He took it back and brought her a dish of plain pasta with a blob of butter on top. The pasta was $35.

The Hermitage means a *hermit's place*, a retreat. *Hermit* to me implied humble. It must have been an aristocratic joke. The Hermitage is a huge elegant structure, blocks long, painted a distinctive pale green, with tall white pillars and gilding at every curlicue opportunity. Visitors ascend marble steps to an imposing entrance. The words *opulent, ornate, sumptuous* are accurate descriptors here. The Roman and Egyptian antiquities were breathtaking, the art collection, world class. Yet with its impressive exterior and its magnificent rooms, many of the palace toilets didn't work. Judy whispered to me she was glad she studied ballet, because she had to do a plié over the bowl and aim. One of the greatest museums in the world: no toilet seats or toilet paper. We chided ourselves for being too "American."

Alcohol was sold from kiosks on the street. A plastic two-liter bottle of vodka, a quick beer, or whatever a Russian might need was there for their convenience. At closing time at the kiosk across the street from the hotel, a drunken young man staggered away with vodka bottles under each arm. An elderly grandmother paused in the street to take a swig from a liter bottle. Nearly everywhere, people drank openly. Of course, not everyone was drinking, but public drunkenness seemed of no concern to passersby. Again, I chided myself for my puritanical American reflex.

Was this the end of Communism? Was this raw Capitalism? The live-and-let-live tolerance left me unsettled. An old woman was passed out on the sidewalk across the street from the Grand Hotel Europe. To me this wasn't freedom. What we saw appeared more like despair. Of course, we were only on the streets and in restaurants. We didn't visit people in their homes or speak to anyone, other than ask for directions from hotel clerks. We did observe. These were people surviving. There were two tiers to the economy, one for foreigners and another for

Russians. I joked that they're trying to get back at Americans for losing the Cold War. It wasn't a joke; Russia's economic situation was dire.

The woman picking us up from the hotel to take us to the St. Petersburg train station felt obliged to perform some kind of tourist duty. She told us that Count Stroganoff lived in a palace we passed. "He had no teeth," she said. "He had meat cut into little pieces. That is why there is beef stroganoff." I already knew that.

At the Moskovsky Railway Station we were ushered through quickly. The well-worn locomotive had a red star and faded gold hammer and sickle emblazoned on the nose. We found ourselves on the train before Judy could get something to drink. I needed to pee. We'd been warned against drinking tap water. I tried to buy bottled water from venders standing only feet away from the train. "*Nyet, Nyet,*" the woman train guard shook her finger in my face, preventing me from making a transaction. She pointed us in the direction of our first-class accommodations.

First class was clean but had seen better days. The upholstery didn't match, and linen doilies on a seat's headrest were from an era when that was considered fashionable, or perhaps necessary. The toilets were locked while the train was in the station. Once the train was out of the city, the restrooms were opened. There was a toilet with a hole in the floor. All deposits ended up on the tracks between St. Petersburg and Moscow. The attendant brought us canned cherry-flavored sugar water. It helped Judy, but only a little.

I was personally excited to be in Russia. We were to be in Moscow for eight days. No question, Russia was beautiful. Between St. Petersburg and Moscow there were dense forests, lakes, and then haphazard towns near the tracks. They had the feel of the *colonias* along the Texas-Mexico border.

What did I know about Russia? Not much, but maybe a little more than the average American. During the Cold War, interest in Russian history and language was considered suspect, even unpatriotic, in Texas. Thirty years before, I had studied Russian history at the University of Texas with Dr. Oliver Radkey, who recalled personal conversations with Lenin and Trotsky. The first semester covered czarist Russia; the second semester focused on the first half of the twentieth century, the October Revolution, and events leading to World War II. I'd read accounts and seen documentaries about the significance of the Battle for Stalingrad.

I treasured Chekhov short stories and plays; enjoyed Henri Troyat biographies of *Tolstoy*, *Chekhov*, and *Catherine the Great*; slogged through Boris Pasternak's *Doctor Zhivago*; and sort of remembered Alexander Solzhenitsyn's *A Day in the Life of Ivan Denisovich*. I loved Russian composers, and apropos of nothing, in the late 1970s I saw Rudolf Nureyev standing outside Lincoln Center in New York City waiting to cross the street. We were the same height, and stood several feet away from each other. Smartly attired in a tailored powder-blue suit with a white shirt and a lemon-yellow tie, he smiled, knowing I had recognized him. I have no idea what event he was dressed for, but as he walked away, I thought he was a really gorgeous man.

Of course, my observations about Russia were limited mostly to what I saw and experienced myself. Once we were in Moscow, the film festival installed us in the Hotel Baltschug Kempinski Moscow, a five-star Swiss luxury hotel not open to the average Russian. The hotel staff included imported workers who spoke English, German, French, and I'm certain Japanese, by the number of Japanese guests. Fortunately, our hotel room was paid for by the film festival because we had to pay for everything else. In 1996, the prices for meals and phone service were shocking to me: a bowl of cold cereal and milk, $28; a two-minute phone call to Los Angeles, $400.

The hotel was across the Moskva River from the Kremlin. We passed St. Basil's Cathedral, the Kremlin, and Red Square several times a day to attend film festival events. The festival headquarters was the Hotel Metropol, a massive historic hotel dating from the early twentieth century.

Much of Moscow had to be appreciated from a distance. The civic and cultural center, St. Basil's, the Kremlin, and Lenin's tomb were well maintained. However, away from the city's center, the czarist architecture that appeared like a finely crocheted shawl from afar, up close the doorways, window casings and filigree were badly in need of maintenance. There was less public drunkenness than in St. Petersburg; however, the scent of urine was ubiquitous. The Soviet-era structures, such as the Rossiya Hotel and the assertively dismal high-rise apartments on the outskirts of the city, made no attempt to brighten or uplift the locale.

Judy and I enjoy walking and discovering a city. On the map we were given, the names of streets were in the Roman alphabet; however, the street names, which adorned the corners of buildings, were in Cyrillic.

We got lost in a city where we didn't want to appear lost. We were instructed not to wear our festival badges on the street.

Perhaps the festival was keeping an eye on us; a film festival van appeared and took us back to Red Square. I wanted to find a shop where we might find something particularly Russian. Near Red Square we saw a female department store mannequin on the sidewalk wearing an army green t-shirt with a red star. Her hand pointed across the street. Several small signs in different languages were attached to the body, one read "Army Surplus." I wanted that t-shirt. We entered the shop expecting to find uniforms but were startled by racks of rocket launchers, crates of artillery shells, and a male mannequin sporting body armor. A burly man examined an assault rifle as if he knew how to use it. We backed out of the shop, and someone quickly closed the door behind us.

What was impossible to miss in Moscow were the long lines of pensioners at the entrance to the subway. The Soviet-era pensions no longer paid enough for them to survive. Each pensioner held an item for sale: a dried fish, a small loaf of bread, an onion, or an article of clothing. The sullen old people appeared resigned. I wonder if the Russians hurrying to catch the subway passed the pensioners the way I pass homeless encampments today.

I saw several films I liked. A tender Japanese film followed an elderly couple, the wife with early-onset dementia, in their last days. A film from a former Soviet bloc country portrayed the near dystopian society following the fall of the dictator. The moral of the story: things were bad before the fall of the dictator; they didn't get any better afterward.

The translators and festival staff weren't being paid much and counted on our generosity. I encountered a bit of anti-American resentment from a young festival translator and an older Russian film producer. I didn't take anything personally. The film producer dismissed anything I had to say, so I didn't try.

We read in the *Moscow Times* that a John Bull English Pub was bombed the previous night. We were aware we were followed everywhere. The Baltschug Kempinski Hotel felt like an oasis from the paranoia I was developing. Judy had a dream that an owl appeared and picked at a thread on her sweater, causing it to unravel as the owl flew away.

As Judy and I stood outside the Baltschug Kempinski waiting for a shuttle to take us to a screening, a sleek Mercedes limo stopped at the front entrance. Mercedes automobiles in Moscow were quite common, but it was rare to see one in perfect condition. Most had sustained some type of vandalism: a missing hood ornament, or a rearview mirror attached with duct tape. The driver of the sleek limo, a massive young man made more so by body armor, stepped out of the car. He went around to the passenger side protected from the street and opened the door for a man who looked as though he stepped out of central casting's version of a rich mafioso don. He wore designer sunglasses, black Italian loafers, black slacks, a black silk shirt, a flashy pinky ring and ample gold chains.

Judy whispered, "The man in black is wearing three wrist watches." Sure enough, three glittery jeweled Rolex-style watches were on his wrist.

The limo driver shielded the man until he was indoors, then returned to stand by the driver's door. An odd ritual followed. Taxi drivers waiting across the street came over to pay their respects.

The festival was chaos. Most of the screenings were an insult to the filmmakers. The films were screened without a mask for 1:85 aspect ratio. Mic booms could be seen. The audio tracks were turned down as a man's bored voice translated everything into Russian, or nearly everything, on the fly.

The high points of the Moscow trip were the museums, of course. At the Pushkin Museum, I was allowed to stand within three feet of a Pieter Brueghel the Younger painting, *Winter Scene with Bird Trap*. Another high point, I was introduced to Tonino Guerra, who cowrote *Amarcord* with Federico Fellini. The low point was, I believed the Russians bootlegged my film. The print of . . . *and the earth did not swallow him* had gone missing before its scheduled screening. The festival was about to cancel the screening when Judy gave the festival director hell for our treatment. She was going to complain to the authorities, she said. The film director stalked off to look for the print.

I leaned over to Judy and asked, "What authorities?"

"I don't know. That just came out."

The film print appeared rather miraculously. They tried to tell me the film had been held up in customs and had just arrived. However, when I opened the film's shipping case, I saw the metal reels had been removed from the film. I didn't believe it was my film. There was colored film leader[9] on the film that I had not placed there.

"Did someone make a copy of my film?" I asked. "This isn't mine."

"Those are not Russian colors," the festival director replied nervously. "This is your film."

"Then where are my film reels?" I asked. The festival director avoided eye contact and said, "I'll see that they're returned." The reels were returned.

The screening went as painfully as expected. There was no 1:85 mask; so yes, mic booms were visible; and the sound was turned down for the same lugubrious translator. I was later informed that when the actors spoke Spanish, the translator said, "Here they are speaking Spanish. I don't know what they're saying."

I suppose I should have been flattered that someone considered the film important enough to bootleg. Judy and I had seen kiosks on the street selling videotapes of American films that were currently showing in first-run US theaters. The artwork on the video boxes had been copied badly, but there they were: *Pocahontas* and *Toy Story* from Disney, *Batman Forever* from Warner Bros., and many other major titles. It was not likely those videotapes were licensed by the US distributors.

The *Moscow Times* said that major renovations were being made to the city for the anniversary of its founding 850 years ago. Moscow was getting a face-lift. There were scaffolds in front of many buildings where plastering repair work was being done by hand on the czarist-era buildings. Women worked alongside men. Maybe a good time to return for another visit would be after they fix the toilets.

Before departing Russia, we were told to leave all Russian currency behind. I didn't. I collect samples of foreign currencies. I got away with about five dollars in rubles. For some reason there were five checkpoints at the airport where our luggage was either x-rayed or opened again. The repeated checkpoints made Judy uneasy.

Once we were home, for the first two nights I awoke from a deep sleep and thought I was still in Moscow. I had to get out of bed, go to the window and look out at my garden until I convinced myself that I really was home.

9.   Leader: A length of blank film spliced at the beginning of a reel to assist in loading it onto a projector to either project or copy.

I was invited to the Viña del Mar Film Festival in Chile, which is as far south of the equator as Santa Barbara, California, is north of the equator. Judy and I stood on a beach where Magellan's ship had landed on the voyage around the world. There were two high points. I met Miguel Littin, the talented Chilean director, and *. . . and the earth did not swallow him* won the Jury Award. The irony about the award was that it was given in recognition that only through doubt in the existence of God can one achieve true faith. That was not what I had in mind in making the film, but okay. I accepted the award. The low point was the screening. One of the projectors broke down and the film had to be shown with pauses to change reels. Fortunately, the audience patiently stuck around to the end.

26

WHAT GOES AROUND

Roosters went into production in 1991, a year before . . . *and the earth did not swallow him.* In 1995, while . . . *and the earth did not swallow him* was screening at film festivals, *Roosters* finally made its theatrical premiere. What had begun as a Southwestern USA Latino production with Chicano actors evolved into an international production with blockbuster ambitions. The producers cast international stars to hedge their bets and assure success. Edward James Olmos was its only American lead. The other four leads were Danny Nucci, Austrian; Sarah Lassez, Canadian; Sonia Braga, Brazilian; and Maria Conchita Alonzo, Venezuelan. Whatever the producers, American Playhouse, or the principals had in mind, the film opened and closed, a critical and financial failure.

Kevin Thomas, of the *Los Angeles Times*, wrote on July 14, 1995:

If Milcha Sanchez-Scott's heavily symbolic stage play about a dysfunctional Latino family in the rural Southwest were to have a prayer of working on the screen, she would have had to jettison her many highfalutin, ultra-theatrical, quasi-poetic flights of fancy. They are at war with both the natural-sounding dialogue that her people speak the rest of the time and with the sheer realism that the camera imposes upon both her work and its authentic locale. The result, it is sad to report, draws considerable unintended laughter.

Why do I bring up the negative review? Not to gloat. I'm fully aware of the compromises I made. I bring it up because it comes back to the empty tokenism that somehow distinct Latino cultures are interchangeable. The film might have worked if they had trusted the poetic flights of fancy. To be fair, the film had fine performances, and good production values.

Then there was National Latino Communications Center (NLCC), and how Jose Luis Ruiz chose to support star-studded *Roosters* and bury . . . *and the earth did not swallow him*. In 1995, at the national PBS/ CPB conference, the NLCC promoted *Roosters* and an upcoming documentary series without mention of . . . *and the earth did not swallow him*. Representatives from NEH and CPB were stunned by the glaring omission. Would I had preferred that my situation with Jose Luis been different? Of course, I tried to be cordial with the man. I had agreed to the rewrite that the NLCC partially paid for so they had a little skin in the game. Paul and I thanked the NLCC and Jose Luis, NEH, CPB, American Playhouse at every event.

The invitations to the Cairo Film Festival and the Havana Film Festival were made through the NLCC. I was asked to supply a print for the festivals, and told nothing more.

A couple of months later when I stopped by the NLCC office to pick up my print, Jose Luis informed me that . . . *and the earth did not swallow him* had won the Cairo International Jury Prize for Best Director. That information would have been good to know in a timely manner. We could have used the publicity. The award was a thirteen-inch statue of Isis, the Egyptian goddess of motherhood, magic, death, healing, and rebirth, encased in a museum-style clear Lucite case. My name and the name of the film were inscribed at the base.

However, I never saw the award in its mint condition. Jose Luis pointed to a three-foot-long box that had been opened to reveal its contents. Sometime, somewhere, the award was smashed in the center with something like a baseball bat or someone's foot. "Isn't that a shame," Jose Luis said, as if he had just discovered the defacement.

I later learned from NLCC staff that when the festival asked for the director to attend, Jose Luis sent Luis Valdez, although . . . *and the earth did not swallow him* was the official festival entry. Luis Valdez had nothing to do with the invitation. As far as he knew, he was there to represent his film, *La Bamba*, which was not in competition.

Jose Luis sent my friend Lupe Ontiveros to the Havana Film Festival. She may not have been told she was there to accompany . . . *and the earth did not swallow him*. I'd known Lupe for over twenty years. She was a pal. From the start of her career, I hired her because she made my films better by simply being in them. The camera loved her.

The next time I saw Lupe, we were chatting until I asked her about the Havana Film Festival. Lupe became visibly jumpy, as if I had caught her shoplifting. She talked nonsense about the opulence of the accommodations and the poverty of the people. She never answered my question and slipped away at the first opportunity. The next time we met at a function she joked about her medical problems, but quickly disappeared. We didn't see each other for a while, as happens in the business. Unfortunately, Lupe's medical problems were no joke. She died before I could tell her I didn't blame her. She didn't take anything from me. I'd have been happy to have her represent the film. She was damn good as the *puta*.

Jose Luis had it in for me, and the only reason I could fathom was that I didn't go through him to apply for open-competition public funds. As one of the first producers I worked with had warned, some guys are spiteful. You can't make them go away, so you have to learn how to go around them. I had gone around Jose Luis, and he was making me pay.

In 1996, when it became known that Jose Luis was being investigated by the FBI, other producers started publicly sharing their grievances. But even after he'd been indicted for multiple felonies, he was still serving on public television panels making recommendations affecting . . . *and the earth did not swallow him*. He ultimately pleaded guilty to misappropriation of funds and tax fraud.

His actions effectively destroyed the National Latino Communications Center (NLCC), financially stranding dozens of producers. The news of his downfall and the failure of *Roosters* could have given me schadenfreude. It didn't. Such failures cast shade in all directions.

That same year, CPB began an affiliation with a new entity named Latino Public Broadcasting (LPB) led by Edward James Olmos. LPB remains the Latino minority consortium to this day.

Before you say "cut," wait five more seconds.

—Wim Wenders

27

THE "VICTORY" LAP

The national television debut of . . . and the earth did not swallow him took place on June 4, 1996. In the leadup to the broadcast, KPBS San Diego and Paul Espinosa were well positioned in the PBS system to handle the campaign. National PBS and local stations did an excellent job promoting the show. Reviews from newspapers across the country commended its emotional power. The downside to the night? Tuesday, June 4, was also the first night of the Chicago Bulls and the Seattle SuperSonics NBA playoff. Not wanting to compete with the big game, the networks ran reruns. The upside? That night, PBS might have been a refuge from reruns and basketball. . . . *and the earth did not swallow him* was the highest rated American Playhouse presentation for the year, even in Chicago. The next important statistic from the Nielson ratings was that the show not only retained its audience, it gained viewers until the end.

Dr. Ricardo Romo, who had been one of the film's NEH academic advisors and was vice provost of undergraduate education at the University of Texas, invited me for a campus screening at UT's Hogg Auditorium. At the reception prior to the screening, Dr. William H. Goetzmann, professor of American studies and also one of the academic advisors, took me aside and enthusiastically related that the president of the university had seen the film and loved it. "He thought it was so much better than the book." That made me wince. Several people had made the same remark. I had such a deep respect for Tomás Rivera, I felt the comparison slighted my friend. I never intended for the film to surpass the source.

Hogg Auditorium was filled to capacity. Dr. Américo Paredes, the renowned historian, folklorist, and musician, was in the front row. Having him dismiss my ideas as "too flashy" years before, I was concerned about how he would react to . . . *and the earth did not swallow him.*

After the screening there was prolonged applause; as I was brought back on stage by Dr. Romo, I saw Dr. Paredes stand and walk toward the stage. He approached slowly, grabbed me, and gave me a hearty *abrazo*, then gave me a big kiss on the cheek. After that, the evening was a blur. I believe the good doctors took me to dinner.

The following morning, I called Mom to tell her Américo Paredes approved of the film. Mom hesitated then asked, "Who's that?" Of course, it was Dad who would have known. There was never one large moment that made me feel I had achieved success. The scenes that didn't get shot were like the deaths of close friends. Small things gave me satisfaction, such as Américo Paredes's embrace, and a letter from a man writing that when he and his family arrived home after seeing the film, they sat around the kitchen table and reminisced about their own family's history.

Because the film had premiered elsewhere, the Cannes Film Festival requested to screen . . . . *and the earth did not swallow him,* out of competition at its program called *Un Certain Regard.* I was proud it was asked. Perhaps the most gratifying invitation came from the Rimini Film Festival. Rimini was Federico Fellini's home town. After the original screening, the festival contacted me asking if the film could be held over for extra screenings. I said, yes.

The person who made my film journey possible was Tomás Rivera's wife, Concha Rivera. I truly hope I didn't let her down. Concha and Tomás's daughters attended the premiere in Riverside, California. There was a reception, and many of the actors were present. The sold-out screening was held at the historic Fox Theater in downtown Riverside.

It was well-known industry lore that when a film was tested "out of town," for the studios that meant the Fox Theater in Riverside. This was where *Gone With the Wind* received its first public screening. The Fox Riverside was created to replicate the experience of USA first-run theaters. The projection and audio systems were state of the art, for 1939. I mention that not to be a snob, but because the theater gave me a fascinating insight.

The powerful sound system made the thunder in the distance viscerally palpable. The film was projected from high up, above the balcony, to a screen far below. The distance and angle created a slight but significant keystone effect to the projected image. The area across three quarters of the upper part of the screen, where an actor's eyes most often appeared, had the sharpest focus. I believe the distortion intensified viewers' response. I heard sobbing and the clearing of throats from the audience when the mother prays for her son missing-in-action in Korea. When the boy discovers the dead body in his bed, 1,400 people gasped as one. As a filmmaker, experiencing that was one hell of a thrill.

Concha Rivera, elegant and gracious, was complimentary. She has always been entirely supportive. The Riverside event was the culmination of years of yearning and planning. I renewed my option with Concha three times before the film went into production. Every cent I paid for the option, and every cent the film accrued to her as royalties, Concha put into the Tomás Rivera Scholarship Fund.

I shook many hands and signed dozens of the programs that evening. An African American woman who had waited patiently in the long queue of well-wishers gave me a big smile and took my hand.

"You probably don't remember me," she said. "I rented you a van in Chino, California, two years ago." I held onto her hand.

"Of course, I remember you," I laughed.

"I told you I was writing down your name. I enjoyed your movie very much. Congratulations."

Because this was a reception line monitored by the university, I found myself shaking hands with the next person in line. The van rental woman was an alumna and knew the protocol. She was gone before I could ask her name.

If you want a happy ending, that depends, of course,
on where you stop your story.
—Orson Welles

ACKNOWLEDGMENTS

Filmmaker's Journey was published with generous support from the Wittliff Collections at Texas State University, San Marcos, Texas. For this honor I thank Dr. David Coleman, director of the Wittliff Collections. I am also deeply indebted to Steve Davis, Wittliff Collections' curator of literature, an early reader whose support and thoughtful notes contributed to this publication.

In 2015, Dr. Frank de la Teja, then director of the Center for the Study of the Southwest, invited me to do a residency at the university. The Wittliff Collections had recently acquired my archives and wanted me to produce a reading of a play and begin work on an essay about my film adaptation of Tomas Rivera's seminal novel *… y no se lo trago la tierra*. I worked intensely, finished a draft of the play, *Speaking of Cats*, and completed a first draft of my novel, *Odd Birds*.

But as for the essay, I made notes and assembled diary entries but avoided dealing with the subject. It took several years before I could understand how making the film cost me, from alternating bouts of excitement and fits of despair. I am indebted to the Center for the Study of the Southwest and the Wittliff Collections for starting me on that journey of rediscovery.

I am grateful to Concha Rivera, widow of Tomás Rivera, for the opportunity of a lifetime, allowing me to adapt Tomas Rivera's beloved book.

Filmmaker's Journey would not exist without the creative input of my wife, Judith Schiffer Perez.

I am thankful for the validating comments from the additional readers: Luis Valdez, Creative Director of El Teatro Campesino; Carlos Rene Perez, my brother and brilliant photographer; Dan Bessie, my old business partner and dear friend; Concha Rivera; Virgil Harper, virtuoso cinematographer; and Mark Rozett, master sound designer.

Finally, I want to thank the entire staff at Texas A&M University Press for a job well done. I appreciated the expertise of Editor-in-Chief Thom Lemmons; Pat Clabaugh, senior editor and project manager; Dawn Hall, copyeditor; Kyle Littlefield, marketing manager and his team; and Kristie Lee and Laura Forward Long, designers.

INDEX

The letter *p* following page locator denotes a photograph.

academic advisors on the National Endowment for Humanities grant: Castañeda, Antonia, 105; Barrios, Gregg, 156; Goetzmann, William H., 106, 173; Hinojosa-Smith, Rolando, 86, 105, 110; Kanellos, Nicolas, 105; Madrid, Arturo, 105; Olivares, Julian, 146; Romo, Ricardo, 173, 174

Aguilar, Josefina: artist in Oaxaca, 38. *See also Monitos*

Alcalá, José (actor), *. . . and the earth did not swallow him*, 134, 142

American Playhouse, 1–7, 86, 103–106, 109, 116–118, 123, 128–133, 142, 143, 147, 148, 151, 155, 156, 158, 160,168, 173

Angie (one act comedy play, 1973), 46

Arau, Alfonso (actor) 59–61

Armijo, Emilio (session musician, accordion), 149

Astronauts and Jellybeans (1977): won Cine Golden Eagles award, 65

Barr Educational Films: Bob Barr owner, film distributor, 69, 75, 79

Barrientos, Adela (piñata) maker, 85

Barrientos, Juan (piñata maker), 85

Bessie, Dan (producer/animator), 22–24, 29, 44, 63, 64–67, 69, 91*p*

Between Friends (1990), 122

Bilingual Foundation for the Arts, 49

Blanco, Teodora (artist): in Oaxaca, 38

Bolton, Jay (sound recording engineer), 148, 150

Bonilla, Art (actor), 140

Brown, Willa (Black aviator), 121–122, 158

Calderon, Tony (producer), 14–15, 21

Caplan, Harry (production manager), 30, 31, 34, 91*p*, 126

Castillo, Enrique "Kiki" (actor), 6, 152

Castro, Sal (high school counselor), 103

CBS, TV network, 65, 69

cherry pickers (special vehicles used in films), 34, 91

Chicano Moratorium March (1970), 48

Cinesound, sound mixing studio, 151, 152, 154

Clark, Ken (director), 14, 19, 20, 24–25

Coleman, Dr. David: director of the Wittliff Collections, 177

Corridos (musical, 1982), 121

Corporation for Public Broadcasting (CPB), 106, 109, 115, 117, 123, 125, 145, 147, 148, 155, 158, 159, 170

Dangcil, Linda (actor), 140

Daviau, Allen (cinematographer), 31, 32, 33, 35, 120, 126

Davis, Bill, illustrator/animator, 65, 68, 151

Davis, Steve, General Editor, Wittliff Collections, 177

Deason, Paul (sound mixer), 20, 23

de la Teja, Dr. Frank: director of the Center for the Study of the Southwest, 177

DeLyser, Femmy (Lamaze instructor), 80
DeHoyos, Nacho, Los Veteranos Bar, 112
Dewell, Michael (agent), 49
Diaz, Albert (photographer *Los Angeles Times*), 7
Dreams of Flying film (1989): won five awards, 103
Dryer, Ivan, 30
Dunn, Reg: general manager of FotoKem, 155

Eastman Kodak Company: *How to Make Good Home Movies*, 11; Ektachrome, 38; price, 40; film use, 122, 126
El Teatro Campesino, 72–75, 131; founded by Valdez, Luis and Valdez, Daniel, 131, 177
Elizondo, Hector (actor), 148
Esparza, Moctesuma (producer), 43, 48, 59–61
Espinosa, Paul (producer), 1, 102, 118, 125, 127, 132, 145, 147, 156, 157
Executive Action (1973), 29, 33, 152; directed by David Miller, 30, 35

Fellini, Federico (director), 10, 145, 147, 166
Filmation animation company, 69
FilmFair Communications: film distributor, 39, 40, 50, 59
Films and filmmakers: early influences, 10
Fleischer, Max (cartoonist), 62
Folioscope, 63
FotoKem: film lab, 25, 65, 155
Fox, Sonny (game show host), 15

Galban, Margarita (director), 47
Ganz, Armin (art director), 128, 129, 131–135, 139–140, 142
Garza, Carmen Lomas (artist), 122–123
Garza, José (amulet maker), 50–51, 92
Garvin, Tom (film festival agent), 156
Geller, Phyllis (vice president KCET nation programing), 101
Gonzalez-Contreras, Geree (session musician, vocalist), 149

González, Francisco (harpist), 74, 149
Guerrero, Evelyn (actor), 140

Hale, Carolyn (associate producer), 134, 140, 143
Harper, Virgil (cinematographer), 5, 97p, 120, 122–123, 126, 128, 132–134, 158, 178
Heard, Howard (editor), 146
Heffley, Wayne (actor), 95p
Hilgard, Adaline (actor), 95p
Heick, Susan (editor), 120, 143
Hein, Frank (artist), 12, 90
Hernandez, Bel (actor), 152
Horowitz, Gary (producer), 29, 31, 32
Hull, Ron, (president Corporation for Public Broadcasting), CPB, 106
Humphries, John: employed at Universal Studios, 67, 68
Hunt Brothers: impact on the price of film, 40

Ice Capades, 25
Inner City Cultural Center, 46, 49
International Public Television (INPUT), 77, 101, 106, 10

Jackson, C. Bernard: director of the Inner City Cultural Center, 49

King, Rodney, 1–3
KFWB (AM), all-news radio, 4, 146–147, 150
KUSC (FM): classical music radio, 146
Kraft, Gabby: employed at Universal Studios, 67, 68

Lancaster, Burt (actor), 29, 31, 33, 34, 90p
Latinos: geographic concentration and influence on media, 116–117
Lauter, Ed (actor), 31, 33
Law, Lindsay: director *American Playhouse*, 116, 118–119, 123, 139, 144–145, 147
Lee, Russell: Depression era photographer, 131
Lee, Ruth (editor), 120
Leib, Carl (photo darkroom instructor), 9

Lerner, Irving (editor), 30, 31–33, 38, 91p;
    director, *Studs Lonigan* film (1960), 32
Lewis, Edward (producer), 29
Llanes, Daniel (first crew), 14
Lieberman, Ernest (composer), 68, 121
López, Sal (actor), 142
Los Desarraigados/Uprooted (1977),
    47–48, 93
Los Quemaditos, 105, 111, 113
Loya, Marcos (composer/musician),
    99p, 85, 121, 144, 148–149

MacKenzie, Gisele (actor), 3
Mancuso, Frank Sr.: president of
    Paramount Studios, 156
Market Place in Mexico/Tianguis (1974),
    58
Medina, Julio (actor), 48
Mendez, Louis (session musician,
    guitar), 149
Midgette Toy Company, 63
Montalbán, Ricardo (actor), 27
Mijangos, Alberto: cultural attaché,
    Mexican Consulate San Antonio,
    50–53
Miller, David: director *Executive Action*,
    30–35, 91p, 126
Morrill, John (cinematographer), 14, 15,
    19, 20, 21, 23–25, 64, 120
Morones, Bob (casting director), 2, 5, 6,
    66, 126, 132, 134, 143, 147, 148
Moscow International Film Festival
    (1996), 160–168
*Mozo: An Introduction into the Duality of
    Orbital Indecision* (1966), 11
Murray, Ben (Sheriff of Dimmitt
    County), 112

National Latino Communications
    Center (NLCC), 115–116, 155, 159,
    170–171
National Endowment for the Humanities
    (NEH), 2, 66, 101, 102, 103, 106, 107,
    109, 110, 111, 116, 117, 119, 123, 125, 145,
    146, 155, 158, 159, 170, 173
New York Filmmaker's Cooperative 13,
    14; accepted *Mozo: An Introduction*
    into the Duality of Orbital Indecision
    (1966), 12
Nosotros, Latino advocacy group: acting
    classes, 46

Olmos, Edward James, 6, 71, 99p, 117,
    119, 171
Ontiveros, Lupe (actor), 46, 66, 85, 117,
    127, 142, 171
Onttonen, Markku: Finnish director,
    160, 161
Ortiz, Bartolo: real person/character in
    film, 44, 111–113, 131

Papp, Joseph (director), 117
Paramount Studios, 156
Paredes, Américo, (folklorist, professor,
    writer), 43, 78, 174
Pearce, Mallory (designer/animator), 64,
    65, 69, 94p
Pennington, Buck (director), 24, 25
Peralta, Robert (session musician,
    guitar), 149
Perez, Carlos Rene (brother, photogra-
    pher), 9p, 89p, 92p, 94p, 97p, 98p, 177
Perez, Estela (mother), 13, 31, 53, 62, 63
    76, 87p, 113, 157, 174
Perez, Judith Schiffer "Judy" (spouse), ix,
    2–5, 15–23, 37–39, 48, 50–57, 65–67, 72,
    73–75, 79, 80, 85, 95p, 96p, 102, 111, 116,
    120, 145, 149–150, 160–168
Perez, Rachel (daughter): wardrobe
    crew, 122, 139
Perez, Rafael "Rafi" (son) (art crew), 2,
    66, 67, 76, 80, 122, 139
Perez, Severo: *See also . . . and the earth
    did not swallow him* (film, 1994);
    Angie (1973); *Astronauts and Jellybeans*
    (1977); *Between Friends* (1990);
    Dreams of Flying (1989); *Executive
    Action* (1973); *Los Desarraigados/
    Uprooted* (1977); *Monitos* (1973);
    *Mozo: An Introduction into the Duality
    of Orbital Indecision* (1968); *Seguin*
    (1982); *Soldierboy* (play, 1981); *The
    Notorious Jumping Frog of Calaveras
    County* (1980); *Tianguis (Market*

Place in Mexico, 1973); *Willa Brown:
An American Aviator* (1996); *Writing,
Plain & Fancy* (1979), *Zoot Suit*, (1982)
Perez, Severo Sr. (father), 13, 26, 43, 63,
67, 76, 133, 156–157
Portillo, Rose (actor), 66, 140

Richard (employee at Reliable Sash &
Door), 83
Rivera, Concha (wife of Tomás), 79, 86,
106, 119, 159, 174, 175, 177, 178
Rivera, Henry (brother of Tomás), 111,
113
Rivera, Tomás: author of . . . *y no se lo
tragó la tierra* (. . . *and the earth did
not part*), ix, 1, 43–45, 65, 67, 78–79,
86, 101, 111–113, 130, 159, 173, 175
Rivera, Tony (brother of Tomás; medical
doctor), 111, 113
Rodney King Riots (1992), 1–7
Rodriguez, Marco (actor), 140
Rodríguez, Miguel (narrator), . . . *and the
earth did not part*, 147–148
Rodriguez, Richard (first crew), 11, 12, 89
Roosters film (1995), 169, 170
Roosters play (1987), 102, 106; Lupe
Ontiveros Lupe, and Pepe Serna
(actors), 117
Rotundi, Joe (session musician, key-
board), 149
Rozett, Mark (sound designer), . . . *and
the earth did not part*, 152
Ruiz, José Luis, 48, 66, 115, 170–171

Salazar, Ruben: Death at Chicano
Moratorium March (1970), 48
Salazar, Val (session musician, *bajo
sexto*), 149
Scarlata, Estela "Piqui" (set designer), 47
Seguin film (1982): written and directed
by Jesús Treviño, 2
Sanchez, Luis (craftsman), 80, 82
Sanchez-Scott, Milcha, 117, 169
Shepherd, Jim (director literature
department, NEH), 106

Sierra Club documentary (1970), 12, 13
Sifuentes, Eddie: knew Bartolo Ortiz, 112
Soldierboy, play, (1981): 67, 72, 75,
96; background, 77; published in
Necessary Theater (1989)
Studs Lonigan film (1960), 32

Tanen, Ned, head of Universal Studios, 67
Texas Employment Commission, 8, 9, 12,
13, 17, 112
*The Notorious Jumping Frog of Calaveras
County* (1981), 65, 68, 69, 157
Tianguis (*Market Place in Mexico*; 1973), 58
Thomas, Kevin: review of *Roosters*, film,
169
Tokunow, Susumu (sound engineer), 66,
120, 126
Tremors (1990), 120
Treviño, Jesús Salvador (director),
Seguin, 66, 2, 48, 66, 77
Twain, Mark: *Notorious Jumping Frog of
Calaveras County*, 65

Universal Studios, 67, 71, 77; 101
Uprooted/Los Desarraigados, play (1977),
47–48, 93

Valdez, Daniel: actor, singer cofounder of
El Teatro Campesino, 13, 66, 71, 131
Valdez, Luis: *Zoot Suit*, play (1978); *Zoot
Suit* film (1982,) 68; 71; 72, 75–76,
170–171; directed, *Soldierboy* (1982), 71
Vasquez, Gus (key grip), 120
Viña del Mar Film Festival (1996), 168
Vlajos, Sam (actor), 142

Walla: film term for the murmur of a
crowd, 152
Willa Brown: An American Aviator
(documentary, 1996), 158
Williams, Bruce (artist), 10
Writing, Plain & Fancy (1979), 65

Zapata, Carmen (actor), 47, 48, 49
Zoot Suit film (1981), 68, 71